WORK OF ART

To Mary

Thank you and best wishes!

Jim [signature]

WORK OF ART
THE CRAFT OF CREATIVITY

JAMES HEGARTY

THE CREATIVE EDGE BOOKS

Also by this author

Guts & Soul: Looking for Street Music and Finding Inspiration

To See: Tokyo Street Photography

New York 1979 1980: Street Photography Lost and Found

WORK OF ART Copyright © 2014 by James Hegarty

All rights reserved. This book or any portion thereof may not be reproduced or used in any manner whatsoever without the express written permission of the publisher except for the use of brief quotations in a book review or scholarly journal.

First Printing: 2015

ISBN 978-1-312-82564-2

THE CREATIVE EDGE BOOKS
WWW.THECREATIVEEDGEBOOKS.COM

To Janet, James, and Anna.

*We are the hands
and the eyes,
the words and the motion.*

*We are the power that transforms imagination
into reality;
the spirit that propels us all
forward.*

Contents

Acknowledgements .... *xi*

Preface: Learning to Fly .... *xiii*

First: Inspiration 1

    Artifact 3

    Fearless 5

    Finding Water in the Desert 11

    The Prophet 17

Second: Discovery 25

    Artifact 27

    Ready? 29

    Exploration 33

    Passion and Significance 39

Third: Development 45

    Artifact 47

    Across the Frontier 49

    Raw Exploitation 55

    The Computer and the Hammer 61

Fourth: Implementation 67

    Artifact 69

    It's About Power Really 71

    Micromanagement 75

    Action 79

Fifth: Completion 83

    Artifact 85

    Speed Bumps 87

    Baked 93

    Keep on keeping on 101

Epilogue: Flying *105*

Works Cited *109*

From the Author *111*

Acknowledgements

It is a scary thing to begin to write, or draw, or compose, or sing.

It takes courage to stand on the edge and realize that whatever comes next flows entirely from one's own imagination.

No matter how determined we are, or how strong our process, at some point our resolve will be tested. And our individual commitment alone will not be enough to keep us from turning away.

That is when it comes down to this: it takes help.

I've always had a lot of help, more than my fair share. It has been my family, my son James, my daughter Anna, and my wife Janet who have supported this work on a daily basis over the past three and a half years and looked out for me, and kept me sane and safe. We all need that kind of help.

I have learned much from the thoughtful discussions I have had with Mary-Jean Cowell, Thomas Zirkle, Hilary Harper-Wilcoxen, and Anna. Several friends have helped along the way as readers of early manuscripts: Steven Thomas, Janet Buchanan, Jeff Bailey, Ben Wann, Lisa Hagan, and Libby Scheiern, as well as Hilary and Anna. Finally, while all responsibility rests with me, Sam Doty and Marla Hansen were immensely helpful with the preparation of the final manuscript.

To all of these people, I express my sincere thanks. This book could not have reached completion without you.

Preface

Learning to Fly

Leonardo da Vinci had a vision that human flight was possible.

He imagined that a machine of wood, leather, and raw silk could flap its wings like a bird to rise from the ground and give us all a higher perspective.

He was a visionary, a genius, a masterful painter, and perhaps the most widely known "Renaissance man" of all time. His interests ranged from physics to natural science, philosophy to art. He was an inventor, a thinker, a sculptor, and a painter; his expertise spanned a vast number of subjects.

He was born in 1452 near the small Italian town of Vinci in the hills that gradually rise above the north side of the Arno River valley only a few miles downstream from Florence. When he was fourteen, Leonardo was sent to Florence to apprentice with the famous painter, Verrocchio. After studying with Verrocchio for six years, Leonardo's father set him up with a studio in Florence. From that point on he worked as a freelance artist and engineer in Florence, Milan, and Rome.

There exist today eleven *Codices* of his written works. Some are loose collections of papers combined into a single package by later collectors. Others are relatively intact journals and notebooks preserved in their original state. Each page is literally crammed with his sketches and unique backwards handwriting – inventions, studies of anatomy, his philosophical thoughts, and ordinary things like how much he spent on dinner.

Throughout his life he was fascinated with flying.

He writes in the *Codex Atlanticus* of his earliest childhood memory: a Kite landed on his crib and flicked his lips with its tail. Leonardo loved birds. He would often purchase them just to set them free from their cages.

By 1505 he was again in Florence, designing and painting a great mural, *The Battle of Anghiari*. Beginning in that year he made drawings and documented his field observations of birds using their wings to maneuver and soar on the wind currents. *The Codex on the Flight of Birds* consists of 18 folios or pages bound with a simple cardboard cover. It is small enough to be carried in a large pocket. This was to be the beginning of an extended treatise on the physical laws that govern the flight of birds and would become the basis for the construction of a flying machine.

It is in his hastily drawn sketches of birds soaring and turning as well as the methodically executed renderings of the anatomy of bird and bat wings that we can perceive the excitement of discovery that he felt as his observations coalesced into a thorough understanding of the properties of flight.

And it becomes clear, over time, that he was unwaveringly committed to the concept that human flight was possible – if only a machine could be designed that was capable of emulating the motion of bird wings.

Creativity is this: it is the courage to envision that first flight, the bravery and determination to stand alone on the edge of the real and to believe in the power of ideas enough that we can jump off into the very air of the unknown – and soar through the currents and waves of whatever happens next.

But Leonardo never actually built his human-powered flying machine, the *ornithopter*. However, others have built it from his design drawings. And it doesn't work.

It was a grand vision, maybe even a beautiful object. But it doesn't fly.

Creativity is not only the ability to conceive of extraordinary ideas but also the willingness and ability to do the real work necessary to develop, enhance, and expand those initial fragments of inspiration into something that actually achieves the full implementation of the potential. A beautiful drawing isn't a flying machine any more than Beethoven's four-note melody is not a complete symphony.

It is the *craft of creativity* that takes us from inception – the initial spark of imagination and inspiration – to completion, the fully formed implementation with all its dimensions of detail, expression, and *functionality*.

Craft is the work we do, the application of skill and resources necessary to actually build something we can all reach out, touch, and use. Craft is the means through which we have the conviction and skill to build something trustworthy enough that we can make the leap into thin air with some level of certainty that this thing is going to work.

But craft is also the foundation of our ability to rise above the never-ending series of challenges and setbacks, the "learning experiences" and often harsh encounters with human limitations that try to pull the whole thing down.

Craft gives us the power to be stronger than all that; craft is the stability and resilience that keeps us standing when budgets and time evaporate or there is nothing holding us up except our own vision. Craft keeps everything in motion even when there's no one else on this planet that believes it could ever be possible to rise off the ground.

Achieving human flight required a more developed vision than simply emulating the wings of a bird. It required research and discovery, new insights, and new tools to achieve the shaping of air pressure that generates the lift to get a child's glider and an Airbus A380 off the ground.

And to be honest, it takes some velocity – not only the power of a couple of very big Rolls Royce engines that just might be lying around, but the momentum of our own energy and determination. We've got to stick with it. We've got to actually grab on to the idea and drag it forward, day after day, no matter how hard it gets. It is up to us to lift the idea higher and to do whatever it takes to get it into the air.

It took me a very long time to learn this and to prove to myself that it works. Ten years of my creative life were devoted to the composition and production of a multimedia opera. I had to confront discouragement of every kind, self-criticism, my own inabilities, and limited resources. It was very hard to keep going over so many years and against just about every negativity there is in the world.

As I struggled to stand up to those circumstances, it became clear that I couldn't do it alone. I needed something stronger than my own human gut strength, ego, or willpower to bring a great work into the world.

Gradually, the source of my endurance and energy shifted. As my own personal momentum ebbed and flowed over the years, something much stronger took over: the real source of the power of creativity is not within ourselves but is contained within the value and purpose of the statement itself. The forward thrust is driven by our deep-seated recognition that the concept – the work's message – is vitally important and has value to the world. The work is its own strength.

When I finally learned to tap into that vein, the ability to maintain forward momentum came from somewhere more reliable and permanent than my own muscle and intellect.

I understand now that within those all-night composing sessions and failed rehearsals, I was doing far more than striving to complete a musical composition. I was developing my craft. Through the opera I discovered methods and systems, tools and support mechanisms, that worked for me in my own individual set of circumstances. I found a craft of creativity that could achieve completion – here and now, within the resources and constraints that surrounded me.

In the decades since those days, my work with jazz musicians and composers, with students and professionals, has shown me that the development of one's own craft is the key to creativity itself. Creativity is achieved by the methods and systems that we establish within our own unique combinations of abilities, experiences, and borders.

Ideas are the spark, the impetus. But there's more to it than that. Ideas need to be transformed into real words and works that soar above the ground and give us all a glimpse of something better, something higher.

This is the craft, the day-to-day work of art, which makes amazing stuff happen.

The chapters that follow look at creativity as a system made of five basic layers or actions. The concepts embedded in these layers are the tools and methods of the craft of creativity.

This is not to say that something as wildly complex as creativity is simply a five-step exercise or a recipe-like outline of cookie-cutter words that are supposed to change the world. Everyone knows it's not that simple, or easy.

Creativity is a highly elaborate and personal action. It moves in many directions across multiple layers, simultaneously. Moreover, it is the result of our own individual circumstances and experience and is as varied and unique as our own identity.

But despite its complex and ethereal nature, creativity actually is not magic and it's absolutely not random. It is made of very specific actions that are interlocked and interdependent.

In these chapters, I share the steps that I followed to learn the craft and to master the art of controlling these fundamental forces of creativity.

So come on! Step up, right here. Hang your toes over the edge. Grab an idea and get to work. Seize inspiration and shape it into something utterly spectacular, something that really can change us.

Something that really can fly!

First

Inspiration

and the craft of invention

*There is a sound in the distance,
Rich, dark colors over the horizon,
Voices around the corner,
A view that suddenly opens on a mountain road.
Expansive.*

*This is the energy that propels all creativity:
Inspiration.*

Artifact

"...it's the ability to keep the bottom on the chair that's about 90 percent of what writing is all about." – Jim Lehrer

It was the summer of 1987 and I knew I was nearing a crossroad. At the time I was just starting to comprehend what it takes to do serious work and I was pushing myself to move to a higher level of artistic expression. The premiere of my opera was still seven years in the future and the concept that I would even attempt such a thing had not yet blipped across my radar.

I happened to glance at an interview in a newspaper that day. Lehrer had just completed a novel and the interviewer was asking how it was possible to work in the fields of journalism and fiction at the same time.

He said that journalism had taught him to write at any time and under any circumstance. He didn't need to "wait for the breeze to come through the window and have the little voices speak to me and all that sort of stuff."

The interview completely arrested me; I remember it vividly to this day, as I stood in my studio with the sunlight filtering in through the window like a spotlight on the page.

What good work that I've accomplished, what truly original and creative work that I've come up with, has been the result of keeping at it – even when discouragement or distractions made it seem like I should give up.

For a long, long time now, this has been my mantra:

Keep your butt in the chair.

Fearless

The momentum of ideas is the energy of creativity.

When creativity works, a thousand million things come together like they never have before. And something beautiful, exciting, functional, and even perfect, emerges out of thin air.

How does this happen? How can something so ethereal, so intangible, result in anything that has any substance at all?

It's the craft of creativity. Whether we recognize it or not, there is a system, a process, a series of actions that line up one by one and one on top of another, that takes us from where we are now to where we all will be in the future.

Some of it is entirely spontaneous, subconscious, and maybe at times even automatic. And some of it is strictly structured and highly intentional – improvisation and deliberation at the same time, on many levels simultaneously.

This is what makes creativity so important: ideas are the source of the real solutions that we all need. If creativity is the discovery and implementation of ideas that make our lives better and lift us all higher, it is absolutely necessary that each idea is developed and implemented to the fullest extent of its potential. We can't afford to lose any of them. Ideas must move out from the imaginable and thinkable to the solid reality of the visible and tangible. It is essential that we get this right. We need creativity to work.

So it's time to get dirty, to actually take it apart and see how the moving parts really should connect together.

It all begins here, with an idea. Ideas are the fuel, the energy of creativity. They inspire us, show us the way, give us the motivation to keep working even when it all seems impossible. Ideas are the atomic structure, the swirling mass of highly compacted energy that triggers a whole chain of reactions that eventually explodes far beyond its initial potential and reaches out and touches everyone. It simply works.

The craft of inspiration is in two parts: the search and the idea. Ideas are the spontaneous result of imagination and inspiration. They happen whenever the conditions allow us to be perceptive.

Ideas are ever-flowing. Stand here with me on the very edge, looking out into the future and you will see that there are more ideas than can be counted – all waiting for me, or someone, to grasp their import, discern their value, and figure out how to implement their potential.

Ideas are the easy part. What the craft of inspiration is about is the search, the means through which we arrive at the ability to see the ideas that are already here, waiting for us. Craft is the way we arrive at a state of perception where we can see them and understand them.

The generation of ideas is the result of commanding our ability to perceive. When we are looking hard enough in the right place, ideas will appear.

The craft of inspiration is this ability to be in the right place at the right time with a vision that knows which idea is the one to hook up with, which one of the infinite number of ideas is worth pursuing, today, this year, now.

And it is completely not random. It is the result of the tangible side of creativity, the craft of inspiration.

Separate the idea from the act of searching. And start looking. Ideas are abstract, ephemeral, unpredictable, spontaneous, and ever-present. The system we use to search for those ideas, however, is entirely tangible, predictable, and reliable.

The craft of inspiration is a deliberate series of actions that lead us to exciting and empowering ideas.
...
Leonardo was a genius. He was a visionary and he had truly innovative ideas. He was amazingly creative in terms of his art. He was a highly skilled painter. He envisioned ideas no one had ever seen before and he made those ideas *real*. His paintings touch us all, raise us up, and inspire our lives. And they are still doing it, FIVE HUNDRED years later. That's powerful creativity.

But the ornithopter? It's a different story.

Even though he had a thrilling idea – the possibility of human flight – he didn't implement it.

It took other truly creative people who were willing to do the work, to figure out how to make something light enough and forward moving enough to generate sufficient lift to actually get off the ground and stay in the air. And then they strapped themselves in and took the leap. They put themselves on the line, no matter whether it meant they would soar through the air or land in a painful wreckage on the ground. They did the work and stood alone with it – upright against the forces of common wisdom that said the work was foolish or doomed to failure.

Creativity is both the vision – the idea of human flight – *and* the real thing – the functional object...an object that actually flies. This two-part action is the real task of creativity. And it starts with parsing ideas, developing a system of idea conception that gives us a tangible way to sort through the many fragments of ideas that touch us on a daily basis.

The craft of inspiration is not only the discovery of ideas, it is the method that allows us to sort through the vast number of ideas that we have and direct our focus on the ones that have real value, that are achievable, and best fulfill our vision.

Consider Leonardo's journals. His ability to capture ideas and see their potential was brilliant and far reaching. All his ideas had the potential to touch humanity in ways that would have changed us all. But he knew he wasn't an airplane builder, he was an artist. Consequently, he justifiably chose not to spend years of his life pursuing the implementation of an ornithopter. Beyond the fact that it may have been impossible given the materials and tools available at the time, he recognized that his talent and skills – his true creativity – was as an artist. The statements he was able to make through the visual arts have had a far greater impact than years of failed attempts at building a machine that flapped its wings and never took off.

The craft of inspiration is not just the spontaneity of great ideas smacking us in the face. It is the coldly calculated rationality of knowing the extent of what is actually possible and finding the point where these two different trajectories intersect.

...

Creativity begins here, with inspiration, the idea – alone and bare. It presents itself in compacted fragments of intensity and it becomes our task to unravel them, to find the loose end and start to pull the string, to work through the knots and to hold together the thin frayed lines. Ideas are supernovas of complexity and intensity. As we open them up, dig into the layers, we see more and more facets of their significance, of the true potential we hold in our thought and imagination.

Inspiration is the result of energy, a type of multidimensional momentum that results from two simultaneous forces: internal vision and engagement with reality – a deep connection to real people in real places doing real things.

Inspiration is what happens when all the walls are down and our vision is focused on the distance. Inspiration is the result of looking harder and longer into the future and away from the ordinary and the conventional.

Inspiration happens when there is no fear. No fear of the unknown, no fear of mistakes, no fear of failure, no fear of being ignored, no fear of being different. Inspiration is the result of uncompromised individuality and self-knowledge. Imagination is living in the here and now but seeing past the clutter of everyday life to the clean, clear edge of future potential.

...

Ideas propel the work forward and keep everything moving together, unified. The idea is the guide, the compass that directs every aspect of our work. The momentum of ideas powers the entire system and guides our craft – our inspiration, discovery, development, implementation, and completion.

Momentum is the result of raw inspiration being impelled by something beyond any external point of reference. It is the force that pushes us to go someplace entirely new, to reach farther into the unknown, to dare to try.

Momentum exists here and now in the core of our vision, our ability to see into the distance and discover what is there, to reach out and grab something entirely new, something no one else has ever seen before.

Expand vision, and momentum will grow.

Momentum is the result of a daily effort to reach out and search, day after day. Keep listening, keep sketching; collect ideas in a notebook, write and write some more. Keep pushing, keep the energy flowing, don't stop even when it seems like nothing's happening, or no one else cares, or the phone isn't ringing.

The craft of inspiration is the methods and means that bring us to our raw ideas. It is about putting ourselves out there, in the open water, into the flow, where we can grab at ideas and then do our best to hang on to them. So step outside, search for fragments of new experience in whatever circumstance is available. Large or small, there is something new happening right now, right here. The craft of inspiration is about the search for the new. It is iterative and strong, driven by practice and enlightened by our vision. The craft of inspiration is the task of our very being, the expression of our individuality, and the realization of our imagination.

...

The craft of inspiration – indeed everything in the work of creativity itself – is the search for the new. It is new thinking and new seeing. It is the result of living upon the edge, the place where the unknown becomes the known.

So do it. Start. Turn the corner. Kick open the door. Step inside. Never look back. It's going to be a thrill ride, an adventure, a soap opera, a ballet, an abstract image, a close encounter with something completely unexpected.

Compared to my everyday reality, this is pretty exciting. How could anyone pass on that?

Bring it on.

Finding Water in the Desert

Imagination is the source of inspiration

Georgia O'Keefe and I are driving through the desert. She's a friend of mine. Although that's not her real name, she is in real life a landscape painter. Big canvases, rich colors, lots of energy and activity, everything's in motion. She lives ten minutes north of the Mexican border.

I look out the window, dry earth and cactus. Hot. For mile after mile. That's all that's out here.

In the days before paved roads and any type of modern transportation, the stagecoach companies built a series of stations along the western routes where the drivers could get fresh horses, and both drivers and passengers could get a meal or spend the night. The presence of a reliable water supply made it all possible.

A few years later, the railroads had the same need. Those old steam engines required a reliable supply of water, too, to make the steam that powered the system. As the railroads were built, a series of water tanks were established in places where water was available, near wells and beside streams, to supply the necessary water at the point where it was needed.

In both these ventures, the system worked because of established structures that could supply the needed energy – in this case water. They succeeded because of the establishment of an organized, reliable set of conditions that afforded the needed resources for the system to remain active and fulfill its intended purpose. People arrived at their intended destination.

Consider this: replace the water with inspiration. Instead of stage coach stations in the desert and water tanks beside mountain streams consider the way-stations of inspiration to be the coffee shops, work spaces, airport terminals, and secret hangouts that provide the necessary opportunity and occasion for us to discover the ideas that will drive our train of inspiration and innovation.

A craft that leads to compelling inspiration is no less simple than the support system necessary to drag steam engines and stagecoaches across the vast expanse of the American West.

It is a deliberate structure that addresses issues of supply and support in ways that are unique and effective, and divides the journey into manageable segments.

The craft of inspiration is a unified system of conscious, deliberate action, too. And it is as unique and purpose-built as the infrastructures of transportation and industry.

So what system of support does your inspiration need? Maybe it's the local coffee shop, a sense of community, the kitchen table, a second floor balcony overlooking the Pacific.

At this point, I have to be able to work anywhere. The part of my life when I could have a place to work and time without interruption is past. But I didn't get to here without a struggle. Early on, I badly needed a very specific set of conditions to get anything done – a place where all my stuff was set up and ready to go. And ear plugs were my friends – they blocked out the noise and distractions, and working at night solved a lot of the problems of trying to find a way to do my work and still meet the enjoyments and commitments of family life. Those were complicated times. But eventually the ability to work stabilized.

After writing thousands of commercial tracks, the rituals faded away and the conditions that supported my inspiration became mental rather than physical. As the result of practice and consistency, it became easier to get myself into the work and to stay there, no matter what was happening around me.

In fact, it really has nothing to do with place at all. It's a state of mind, a way of thinking, a zone, a hyper-consciousness that gives us the ability to close out the ordinary and concentrate on the future, on the new – to keep our vision focused ahead, looking out from the very edge.

...

By trade and training, I am a composer. When I started writing, I thought that my ability, my craft of composing, would immediately transfer over to this new endeavor. It didn't. For me, finding a craft of writing was like starting over from the very beginning.

My first attempts began randomly in the stolen moments of Saturday mornings as I waited for my daughter to finish a class. It was a complete struggle. The progress was painfully slow and uninspired. It was clear that I was standing upon the threshold of a long and complicated journey.

But I kept at it for the whole semester. And occasionally I had a day when something good actually happened.

It was here, more than ten years ago, now, that I began to take apart this creativity thing and ask some questions I should have considered years before. Questions like "where does inspiration come from?" and "what do you do with it?"

The answers were complex and often not very precise. Over several years, I mastered the ability to write through a slow experience of trial and error. In the end this is what emerged, a conviction that creativity is a system.

It is a craft that is reliable and replicable, that can be applied under a wide array of circumstances. The quiet solitude of a college library on a sleepy Saturday morning is not required, at all. Inspiration, creativity itself, can happen anywhere under whatever set of strange and challenging circumstances we find ourselves. Creativity does work and it is up to each of us to master the craft.

...

Georgia O'Keefe and I are driving again. The road is starting to climb out of the valley, there's a switchback or two, the vegetation is getting thinner, the earth more barren and covered with more and more sharp rocks. In the rear view mirror I see the valley falling away behind us.

We level off, round a bend in the road. And in the distance, amid nothing but dusty brown-grey soil and rock is a thin band of dark green. As we drive in and out among more bends in the road, the green patch grows larger and wider.

For nearly 50 miles we've driven through a monochromatic wilderness of open space, surrounded by distant grey mountains. And now, as O'Keefe and I drive forward the world suddenly turns green and lush of foliage. It's shockingly beautiful for the sharp contrast and abrupt transition.

I pull off the road and O'Keefe and I get out of the car.

We have stopped, amid the green surroundings of an oasis in the desert, in front of the Vallecito Stagecoach Station. And it is suddenly 1852.

We've been driving a paved two-lane winding road northwest out of Ocotillo, California – a town named for the tall spindly cactus that uniquely grows in this elevation and climate. The road is not marked, but later online I learn it is designated state route S2, the Great Southern Overland Stage Route.

This station was a stop on the first official transcontinental route. It served the San Diego – San Antonio Mail Line, The Butterfield Overland Stage Line, and the caravans heading west on the Great Southern Route.

The Butterfield Overland Mail Route carried mail and passengers from two eastern cities – Memphis, Tennessee and St. Louis, Missouri – west to San Francisco, California. In a very tangible sense, I know that I have been here before, having made several St. Louis/San Francisco runs over these years since my family got scattered across the country. But the *deja vu* is more than a phenomenon of contemporary travel. It is the perception that fills me when I know I have crossed a threshold – opened a door and entered into a new level of understanding, a broader and more inspired vision.

I feel the need to stand motionless, to listen and look, to take it all in, to absorb the impact of space and isolation that only the deserts of the American West can hold.

It's penetratingly quiet, there's no one here, and we stand amid the absurd abundance of vegetation as if we have arrived transported to another planet. I imagine that I have just stepped down from a stagecoach after a full day's journey upon a dry hard road. Instantly, the power of this new perception hits me: the spirit of inspiration is as a well in the desert.

Stop. Drink it up. All of it.

In this story, we have arrived at the place of inspiration, the place in thought that forges the new, that shapes ideas that will build innovations capable of changing reality. This place, in a very tangible sense is where we all must go to find our inspiration, to find ideas that stand in sharp relief to the conventionality of the present. Just as the green vegetation stands in sharp contrast to the cracked and broken rocks and dusty soil of the desert, our ideas, our inspiration are completely apart from the terrain of life as we know it.

The inspiration that leads to powerful ideas is the search for a vision that is as startlingly different from expectations as the oasis is to the desert that surrounds it. Our imagination, our craft of inspiration actually is an oasis amid the conventionality of everyday existence. It is lush with the richness of an entirely new perspective, vivid and inspired with the perspective of ideas new and invigorating.

The oasis where inspiration happens, the conditions that foster the generation of stunning ideas, is a mental place full of the energy of abundance and possibility. It is the place where the new begins; it is the place where the old is left behind.

We get back in the car and head towards town, back across the dry solitude of the desert. The road has changed. I know where it leads now. It is shorter, faster, it is less mysterious. I remember each series of turns. Even though I can't see them, I can drive fast because I know what's coming. I know the system, I know the craft. It's working.

Traveling this road again will be faster, more sure. After a few more trips, I'll even stop hitting the potholes.

The craft of inspiration is a systematic approach to understanding our own needs and the development of ways to meet those needs, to fuel the system. Just as the stage coaches needed water and a cool place to refresh the horses, our inspiration needs fuel and support, the opportunity to soak up the abundance of a unique vision, and the strength of a sure set of way-stations that give us the confidence to set out across a barren landscape, alone. Knowing that a well of fresh water – inspiration – is waiting a day's journey ahead makes it seem a lot more likely that we'll survive the trip across the sharp edges of uncertainty that stand before us.

With deliberate effort it's possible to learn to work within any set of circumstances. It may not be ideal or particularly comfortable, but inspiration can happen anywhere.

It's not the place or the time, it's the freedom – the willingness to let imagination go and fly free.

The Prophet

Wisdom and clarity shape inspiration

My first real friend in St. Louis is by trade a journalist, a Latin scholar, and writer. I call her The Prophet because that's what she is.

As a journalist, she naturally possesses a highly refined ability to cut down to the bone. She knows how to get right to the core of what's going on, to assess whether an idea has any value to the world, and to envision the best way of expressing that value through tangible connections to a community.

When, where, what, why? It seems simple but there's a talent to being able to actually do it. And she really has it.

For the seven years we worked together, she taught me how important this kind of immediacy is to the vitality and success of any project. Starting with the very same questions that drive every dimension of our media-saturated world puts any inspiration and any idea on an immediately sure foundation. These concepts have proven powerful in the communication of work no matter what the content is – a news story, a symphony, or an art novel.

Before I met The Prophet, I had done three productions of my opera and a workshop performance of a multimedia piece. It was a start, but I really didn't have the knowledge or the vision to know what to do next.

When we worked together, The Prophet's wisdom and insights gave me a new strength of determination that it just might be possible to accomplish some really big things. Her knowledge and wisdom helped, but more importantly she was a trusted friend who gave me huge doses of encouragement that helped me believe in the value and worthiness of each project. Her support gave me the ability to expand my perception and to reach for a higher level of scale and excellence. The Prophet helped me do things I didn't think were possible, to really expand my capabilities and reach for a higher plateau.

She was a silent collaborator and together we made a series of increasingly stunning productions. Over the course of seven years, we produced two operas and three multimedia music/theatre works.

Those years were a period of intense creative activity and inspiration. New ideas were constantly in the development pipeline and a large number of collaborators were actively contributing to the energy level. It was a workshop environment that gave me the opportunity to test, explore, develop and refine my individual creative craft. It was here that I really learned how to work, how to make really exciting, dynamic statements.

The story of Risk and The Prophet:

That was what made it all happen. An ability to approach the risk of failure without fear. I could do that because I knew The Prophet had my back.

That really was the key to the success of it all. I could risk doing crazy out-of-this-world stuff because I knew she was covering me both financially and artistically. I knew I could trust her to come to my rescue and not let me fall. I knew I could trust her to still be my friend even if I totally failed. She was an amazing, one-of-a-kind person and those years we worked together, before I went off to chase a rainbow that evaporated the moment I touched it, were the most spectacular years of my professional career so far.

Everyone needs an executive producer.

Everyone needs The Prophet.

Dragging work to ever higher levels of scale, excellence, and community engagement is beyond the ability of one person alone. Moreover, no one I know has the kind of unflinching confidence it takes to keep doing this highly competitive stuff day after day without crumbling occasionally. But to keep going, it takes the ability to bounce back after you've been hit, to knock on every door another time even when there's a really big hairy mean monster on the other side. It takes someone, at least one other person, who is willing to give unreserved support and encouragement to the completion of the idea.

For me, then, it was The Prophet. And that's how the stuff got made.

...

I was scheduled to present a concert-length work at the Contemporary Art Museum in St. Louis in the spring of 2002. During the previous summer, as I began to envision the project, I became fascinated with the concept of the juxtaposition of technology and historical artifacts.

Years earlier in Europe, I'd seen structures built from the ruins of centuries past. Original parts were retained and the missing parts were replaced with new materials. They were a mix of old and new. Fragments of original walls, roof, windows, and doors were preserved and the voids were filled with steel and glass – very contemporary, cutting edge materials juxtaposed upon ancient stonework.

Now known as *parabuilding* in the field of architecture, such buildings are the result of grafting a new addition upon or in association with an older structure. The term was coined by the late architectural critic Herbert Muschamp in 1999.

Muschamp defines the term in ways that accounts for all the shades of meaning contained in the Greek prefix, *para*. The modern addition exists not only beside or related to the original structure, but it may also be in complete contrast and antithetical to it. The combined elements can work together or in opposition. When Muschamp's concept is successful, the combined elements work together and the result is a useful and inspired expansion of the character of the existing historical building.

But when the concept fails, the result looks simply inappropriate and stupid – as if the addition is a parasite upon the "host." In this style, the host building, the historical element, is either enhanced or rendered insignificant by the treatment of the relationship, the scale, the context, or the purpose.

This is useful revisionist theory. At the time however, I hadn't even heard of Muschamp or his terminology. But the theory is a useful means of looking back and sorting through a practice that was happening on the ground in real in a variety of media at the time.

Clear reflections of this concept started to appear in many different manifestations beyond architecture – the world of vintage fashion, the use of color and effects in video, new trends in literature such as graphic novels, and the use of industrial technology to execute classically inspired images in the visual arts.

There's an acid trance beat happening in the next room and down the hallway someone is strumming a lute.

And in the perception of the moment the references combine.

But it's not some new-age-y version of fusion of east and west or north and south. It's not fusion at all. The seams are clearly visible and there's no blending going on.

Call it a flying saucer that landed on the Acropolis. Or a vision of the future: Chicago's Soldier Field or the new entrance to the Brooklyn Museum of Art. No matter which side of the aesthetics the work falls – transcendent or stupid – the result is all about the interplay of the discontinuity of materials and the contrast of reference and significance between the contemporary content and the historical artifact.

Risky. Completely and pervasively.

And that's the whole point.

That pronounced intersection of old and new is fascinating because it interjects the creative uncertainty of contemporary idioms on top of the established solidity of classical forms and vocabulary.

I feel good.

In my day job at the time it was all about sampling and looping. And I was beginning to connect the dots. Using James Brown horn hits and classic R&B beats as the nucleus of entirely new Rap and Hip-Hop musical compositions is fundamentally the same concept as dropping a vintage mid-century handbag on an urban street outfit or a glass and steel entrance on a Greek Revival façade.

Where I was going was trying to discover how these concepts of cultural interaction – the technological juxtaposition of cultural artifacts – could become the unifying and identifying factors in something beyond the current popular forms. I wanted to apply the idea to a large-scale concert work.

The premiere of a new work is always uncertain. Add in the fact that if it falls stylistically outside the mainstream, outside the realm of expectation, uncertainty is drastically multiplied. Moreover, if no name recognition or branding can be associated with the project, there really is nothing to lend a level of tangibility to the audience's expectations.

Historical context is very heavy. History is a strong presence. It carries a lot of significance, a lot of deep, rich associations.

History commands respect.

Respect by context.

I began to search for potential musical artifacts, to seek inspiration in the depths of the past. I had no way of knowing that the work would eventually become aligned with one of the most significant historical events of my time.

...

September 11, 2001 happened.

Devastating. Life changing. The end of an era and the beginning of a new, harder, meaner, more suspicious time. In a sense, the world came of age that day. Like the day my dad passed when I was 39, I never felt like a real adult until he left the stage.

We're all adults now. Grown up. All the poetry about the sky never being so blue again, or the grass as soft is completely true. Just as when he passed, and then a few years later with my mom, joy just isn't the same. Excitement and enthusiasm just fell away. We don't open our door and smile anymore. We crack it open and check around the corner. A lot of old ways ended that day and we all collectively lost something very precious.

I couldn't work. And it wasn't just me. No one could do much of anything. I walked around on autopilot. And so did everyone else. For a long time. There just didn't seem like any reason left in the world. There was never any conscious decision to put the project on hold. It just was.

Slowly the realization that the spring performance was approaching began to sink in. I knew I didn't want to cancel. So I had to work. And I did.

Before the attacks my research had led me to the idea of creating a new version of the opera, *Euridice*, composed by Jacopo Peri. This work was premiered in Florence in 1600 and is considered history's first true opera. It marked the beginning of the Baroque period in music and established the basic form and practice of the first period in the development of opera. It is a reworking of the ancient Greek myth of Orfeo and Euridice and their descent into Hell. It was a work heavily laden with historical significance and classically grounded.

The original opera was produced as part of the wedding celebration of Enrico IV to Maria de' Medici. Because it was performed at such a joyous occasion, the librettist, Ottavio Rinuccini, give a happy ending to the well-known tragedy. In the end, Orfeo and Euridice return to the natural world and are restored to life. They survive their journey into Hell.

In the months after 9/11, the reworking of this story into a collage of contemporary new compositions and authentic recreations of the historical material became a touchstone for me. Clearly, the subject was more than poignant. It was the dream we all shared – to descend into our own Hell and bring all those innocent lives back home and restore the world to what it once was.

It was truly inspiring. I wrote the entire 90-minute work in a six-week period. Now titled *Euridice Remix*, it became an entirely new composition grown out of the roots of the original opera but molded and fashioned into a modern statement using current technological tools. Like fragments in a collage, these musical elements function representationally as well as structurally and as content. I retained the original Italian for passages that were drawn from the original work. English was used for the texts that are completely new additions. The primary purpose of *Euridice Remix* is a musical statement and I did not feel compelled to thoroughly portray all aspects of the story.

There were three performances. The first was on the campus of the college where I was teaching at the time. Two performances followed immediately at the Contemporary Art Museum in St. Louis. The performances were a sell-out. I have never before or since given concerts with standing room only, but these were. People were standing in the aisles, around the sides of the room, and packed against the back wall.

The work, its voice and its message, resounded collectively within us all. It expressed something we all wished and it said something we all wanted to say. It was a collective expression of deepest emotion. It was an extraordinary moment. It was unifying, it spoke to a deep and passionate collective desire, it was big and bold, it had historical depth, it was rich and full, and it was loud and inside each one of us like no number of Marshall stacks could ever be.

It was the power of one idea.

It was the power of inspiration.

…

The craft of inspiration is the search for new insights and thoughts *followed by* the conscious action that shapes those discoveries into powerful, fully formed concepts.

It begins with one powerful idea. Ideas are the product of thought released from the limitations of the world and set free to move beyond conventionality where they cross the threshold of the new.

These creative concepts are the power of ideas made real and permanent. It is the entire creative work that brings these concepts into real existence through the craft of discovery, development, implementation, and completion. Through the strength of a unified system, the full potential – the full significance and impact – of ideas, of inspiration, will be made real.

Ideas are the most powerful thing there is, the most powerful force there is in this world. But they need to be developed, molded, refined. The craft of inspiration is the method that realizes the potential of ideas.

Ideas provoke. They poke a nerve and jolt us into an electric response. We're paying attention now. And we're reacting, we're changing. Passion, intensity, bigness, energy, immediacy. Maybe it's poignant insights or a highly charged rant. Maybe it is a life changing spectacle or the quiet voice of closest intimacy. Maybe it's a completely new way to interact with the world. Inspiration is about immediacy and visceral reaction – it's shock and awe in a very real and personal way.

Powerful ideas leave us blown away, sent home to rethink our lives. They hit us in the gut, the head, and the heart.

Inspiration is deep. It's hugely significant. Inspiration touches hearts, in ways that nothing else can. Inspiration is powerful, more powerful than even devastating tragedy; it has the power to renew, to heal, to restore – even when the world seems torn apart.

Inspiration lights a fire that burns in the hearts of everyone that it touches. It carries us all forward into a better day.

Inspiration is the energy of creativity, the spirit that moves against the impossible and breaks the chains of our own and the world's limitations. Inspiration is at once beyond this world and infinitely rooted in it; it is far above the confines of material existence and it is at the very heart of the human condition. Inspiration guides, guards, leads, moves, propels, and changes us all. It is that powerful. The energy contained in one idea is sufficient to turn the world. We've seen it happen in tragic and magnificent ways. Human invention, machines, enterprise, art – these things can't change the world, ideas change the world.

The power of thought, the power of ideas alone can change us.

That's the significance of inspiration.

Second

Discovery

and the craft of exploration

There are expeditions grand and not,
We step outside and it is ever new.
Discovering the beauty and potential that lies inside an idea is this:
The search for intensity, impact, and meaning.
Significance.

Artifact

Good composers don't borrow, they steal. – Igor Stravinsky

Uniqueness, originality, is exciting. It's thrilling to bring something completely new into the world.

But stealing? What does Stravinsky's famous quote mean in the context of originality? His statement seems counterintuitive, considering the level of individuality he expressed in everything he did. It would be hard to name a composer more original and innovative than Stravinsky.

If I borrow something, I intend to take care of it and make sure I can return it in the same condition as when it was loaned to me. I'm that kind of guy, I guess. It just seems right to treat other people's stuff with care and respect. I'm going to make sure that it doesn't get broken and I'll fix it – restore it to its original condition – if it gets messed up.

However, if I steal something I'm taking it for keeps, and I'm not ever giving it back. It's mine now. To do with as I please.

I'm going to mess with it any way I want: break it, stomp on it, twist it, and paint it any crazy color I choose.

Turn it into something completely new. Change it into something that I want it to be.

Yeah, I've stolen it. It's mine now.

Ready?

Creativity is the search for a vision ever higher.

Creativity is an action. It is an operation. It *moves*.

When everything comes together, the work, the product, the art, the idea changes everything around it.

For me, that's what it's all about: ideas that bring about real change.

…

Let's start here. The deep prep. This probably goes without saying; this stuff is fundamental to just about everything that goes on in the world. You've been here before, I'm sure.

Clean house. Start fresh. Drag all the mental baggage out to the dumpster. Put all the distractions away. Really do it.

Get the tools together, learn some skills, collect ideas, brainstorm, jam, keep the lights on, pay attention, network, keep your chops up. Do the maintenance.

Clear a path. Get all the unnecessary mental clutter out of the way so there's nothing to trip over.

Think, imagine, dream, enjoy. Open any door, don't eliminate any possibility.

Know yourself thoroughly. Take the time to do this. It's essential. Your ability to know what you are really about is the true source of creativity and originality.

Discover your mantra. Compose your manifesto, explain clearly why you are here.

Figure out how you're going to identify success when it hits you in the face.

Do the prep.

Be ready.

...

This is intense. Amazing things happen daily. There's raw power and penetrating insight in creative work. It's full of insane amounts of energy and momentum.

And it's unrelenting; the search for inspiration can get demanding. It's an adventure, it's a wild ride.

So take care of yourself. I mean this. Don't get burned. Live, breathe, eat. Keep a perspective on it all. Keep yourself healthy, keep yourself sane. Keep yourself from falling.

...

I'm still not the master, but I've climbed to the top of the mountain a few times and looked around. The search for real creative inspiration isn't going to fit into ten easy lessons.

But here's a start. Call it a pencil sketch, an outline that you can fill in later:

1. Define some terms – get everyone on the same page.
2. Look around, ask questions, observe, read, study, research – know the field.
3. Prepare the space, tools, skills, knowledge, identify resources and talent.
4. Experiment, go exploring, search for new materials, methods.
5. Collect material, collect ideas, collect content.
6. Evaluate, find connections.
7. Make some decisions, choose a direction, make some plans.
8. Get to work, go do it.
9. Evaluate, test, try every alternative – what's working, what's not, why not?
10. Make mistakes, fix things, change course. Make corrections.

11. Revise, revise, revise; refine the details, reach for a high standard.

12. Finish it! Don't get trapped in an infinite loop of revision; deadlines are your friend.

...

Above all else, remember this:

The product, the work, the art – these books, songs, images, movements, words…these things of themselves are not the message at all.

They are the medium, the tool.

They are only the form, the means through which something much deeper is expressed – the inspired idea, the very underlying vision itself.

A glimpse into an entirely new world.

An original thought.

Communicated.

Exploration

Dig deep, reach out, look harder, keep at it.

As practical and comfortable as the aisle seats are, given a choice, I usually go for the window.

I want to take a look.

I want to see something new.

I want to see something no one else has ever seen before.

And I've seen some amazing things. Heading out of O'Hare towards New York one early morning, the Chicago skyscrapers stood like the gigantic iron towers of another planet as they floated on a blanket of ground-level fog. Flying into Atlanta for a layover recently, the summer storm clouds blocked our flight path. Thirty thousand feet tall, we flew in and out among these enormous formations like a tour bus gawking at the monuments. It was beautiful, majestic, and grandly inspiring.

Flying west towards LA over the Sonoran and Mojave deserts is always a lesson in expansiveness. And then there's Mt. St. Helen poking through the clouds on a trip to Seattle a many strange years ago – a still vivid reminder of the hopes, dreams, and great expectations of a young man who had absolutely no way of knowing just how long and winding and complicated the road ahead would be.

Where are you? Are you standing on the summit of a Colorado 14er? Or on the 98th floor of the Hancock Building? Are you comfortably sipping a complementary beverage while looking out the window of a commercial airliner at 39,000? I'm imagining the view from the space station. I want to go. I want to see that.

What do we see? What montage of images and experiences are establishing the point of reference for our work?

What collection of impressions, snippets of conversations, pieces of art and literature and history, views of the world, and catalog of most secret and personal dreams make up who you are?

Is the view satisfying? Is it colorful enough? Is it exciting enough, expansive enough? Is it wide and rich and deep enough? Is it consistent and thorough enough, or strong and powerful enough?

Is it all those things? There's always more.

Get out of here. Go somewhere, anywhere. Take a walk, take a train, take a plane, take a road trip, get on a boat, it doesn't matter. Go places, anywhere, it doesn't have to be exotic – Delhi or Rio. Eat something new, listen to something new, read, search the Web. Meet people, anyone. Have a conversation, hear a new voice, listen to new dreams, listen to new sounds and rhythms.

Crack open the seal, let something dangerous out of this box we call life.

...

Ideals, dreams, and perhaps even hope itself. These are serious and intense words. Words that really mean something. Not just simple words that mean other simple words. These words mean something tangible, they mean something deep. They are a part of real people, a part of real people's lives. They are the core of who we are, who we want to be and what we want to do.

These are words that people don't ignore or casually accept. Talking about these things is serious, deep, passionate stuff. Don't push my hope or my ideals around. It is a very delicate and potentially scary thing to look in the mirror or to look out of a window. Messing around at this level is stirring the roux, the very fiber of what we do.

It probably seems safer to leave these things alone.

But whether we want to look or not, one day the window shade is going to break and it's going to be impossible to ignore the view any longer. That's when things like this will start to float to the surface: images, sounds, a memory here and there.

Logic and order and reason might not jump in, but over in the corner of the frame something will start to make a little sense, a few pieces of the puzzle will start to match up.

At that moment, things become different. There's unity, relationships, interconnections that were there all along but for whatever reason just didn't seem to matter or were just a little too blurry to get noticed. It's one of those moments when the Tetris blocks all fall into place *on their own* and it seems a little strange.

It can be disturbing.

In a good way. But unsettling nevertheless. Things get bumped, moved around, shuffled, rearranged. The order of stuff changes, the priorities and the to-do list get jumbled up. Maybe it's time to turn left, or turn right. Maybe back up and retrace a few steps.

That moment when whatever has been going on, for no real reason, finally makes some sense.

Why do we do things? Why is anything the way it is?

Maybe it just works. That's good enough, isn't it?

I wanted to do good stuff. I wanted the work to be strong and valuable. I wanted to be sure that the work I did attained a high level of quality. I wanted the work to show that I could deliver the goods and that I had skill.

But did I care if it had any real purpose? Did it matter to me if it had any real underlying foundation in the depths of the earth? Did it ever enter my mind that the stuff had to *mean something?*

No. In retrospect, I didn't care about any of that. For better or worse, for whatever the outcome may have been, I will admit that things were pretty simple then.

Cool idea.

Do it.

That was enough for me. It works. Stuff gets done, cool stuff gets made.

And people dig it.

Just throw the stuff out there. See if it floats. See what rises to the top. Let the market decide. That kind of attitude works. If you're willing to accept that maybe more times than not the stuff is going to sink into the muck.

Early on, that's ok. But after awhile everything gets more complicated. Time, *every* resource, starts to seem more precious. Success brings more opportunities. It gets harder and harder to turn stuff down. Now, all of a sudden the inefficiency of a shotgun theory turns into a liability rather than a business model.

One day, someone says something like, "Why is your work always so, um, colorful/dark/loud/soft/ugly/beautiful?" And it's a friend, who really cares. Maybe someone who really wants to know because she really likes you but just can't understand your stuff at all.

What do you say? How do you answer?

I like it? I wanted to do it that way? I don't know?

So you make something up. And it sort of sounds stupid or doesn't make any sense or doesn't really explain anything.

And she walks away.

Ouch.

Or worse. It's a producer, or a curator, or a collaborator you really admire, or a sponsor, or an investor, or an agent (as it was in my case). Someone who is really interested and has a lot of hope that your stuff could be the next big thing. But, see, in this world of reality we find ourselves in today, that person needs more than hope.

She needs something real because she's going to jump out of the window with you on this project.

This agent, this producer, this whoever needs to feel like the decision to devote time, commitment, and resources in your direction has at least some logic to it. She needs to feel like it's going to be a good thing to fall through the sky with you. She needs to be pretty sure the landing's not going to be so rough it pulls down her mortgage payments and the lease payments on the Maserati. Not to mention her kid's school bills.

Good work counts.

Good work starts the conversation.

Without good work, nothing's going to happen.

Without good work, no one's even going to make a pass at you.

But if they do, eventually there is some talk. And what do you say? There's got to be a strong and identifiable sense of an underlying foundation to the work or there won't be much of a conversation. There needs to be something to hang a relationship on.

"Cool" only gets you so far.

...

The craft of discovery is a method of knowing. It is the way we uncover the true full potential of an idea. Through discovery we test the viability of potentials and we reason with the consequences. It is a force that is always pushing at the boundaries, reaching out, rising higher, expanding the view.

The craft of discovery relates to everything – the community, venue, purpose, vision, and the function. The craft of discovery develops the initial concept into greater dimensions, expands the potential reach and impact, and envisions higher levels of power and effectiveness. The craft of discovery grasps the initial concept and extends it into a larger scope and point of reference than initially perceived.

It is the way that we know the power of the idea that stands before us. It brings us into its trajectory so we can fulfill, complete, the vision that originated it. The strength of innovation is our vision and inspiration but it is our wisdom and determination that are the power that brings the idea to completion. Discover that power and build out from it to bring the idea into the place where it can be entirely complete.

As much as the craft of discovery is about looking out and seeing more and more of this magnificent culture we live in – the details and color and light and people – it is also very much about looking inward, too. It is about seeing ourselves with accuracy – our strengths and opportunities, where we fit in, what we're really doing, what we *should* be doing. It is an almost detached observation of ourselves as we work and function. What's good for us, what suits us? What jacket feels right and doesn't make us look too fat or too skinny? What vocabulary, what set of initiatives, what collection of references and associations work best to achieve the fullest representation of who we are and what we hope to accomplish?

What should we be doing? *Right now?*

What do we know that no one else knows, what have we seen that no one else has ever seen?

What significance can our work have, what impact can we make? What can we do to raise us all up higher?

Look out the window. Think about it. Ponder the potentials *and* the realities.

What can each of us do – that no one else could ever do?

There's something there. Look again.

That's the target, the focal point of the craft of discovery.

Above all, don't get distracted, or look away. Set the focus of discovery sharply on this and lock it down.

Seriously know this.

Passion and Significance

It's not about the notes, the colors, or the words; it's what they say that really matters.

This is about looking hard, mining ideas for their full potential – discerning the full significance of an idea.

Discovering, looking, looking harder and closer.

A window is the means of capturing a vision, a way to see through the wall, to see beyond borders, past barriers. A way to see something no one else has ever seen.

This is about uncovering the entire reality of an idea. This is about knowing and understanding the idea in its complete magnitude.

...

I am standing in a train station. It is Paris. It is Tokyo. It is New York. It is Venice and I am waiting to leave. Why? Because I have to. The last touch, the last look into her eyes, the last time I heard her voice on the other end of the phone, the last time I felt the brush of her hair all have some kind of mystical power to linger, to remain suspended in bullet time. I'm standing on the platform spinning thoughts around and trying to examine the details from all perspectives at once. Trying very hard to impress those moments into some kind of silicon database that will never be erased or lost.

A journey begins and ends. Each day is a step further along the path. The doors open and another platform appears. Trains enter and passengers exit. Sometimes I board the train, sometimes I let it go. Another will follow shortly. Maybe the destination is wrong, somehow. But how do I know this?

There's a large dose of mystery in all of it. A picture, a feeling, or an atmosphere. I want to be transported, I want to be a passenger sometimes. I want to step off the platform into the thin air of speed and go somewhere. A new place that moves me, makes me think, reconsider, revise, renew. I want to be up-ended, turned inside out, rearranged. I want to read Kanji, or at least think I can. I want to find out that it's different inside someone else's head and I want to know more about that. I want insight, I want a vision. I'm in love and I don't know why. Isn't that the best kind of love? The most intense? There isn't any reasoning any more, there's just being, there's just lovemaking, and if I'm totally honest, there's a lot of fantasizing about it. There's reality, and then there's everything else. It's the "everything else" that's fascinating.

It's as simple as that. *Leaving Venice* is leaving no one, no place, and it's leaving a special place and a special person. You decide. It's a complete fiction and it's the only reality.

How do you address the sensual? If significant work is about the exploration of the human condition and our collective relationships in this thing we call modern life, at some point the camera is going inside places that won't end up suitable for younger viewers. How hot and steamy or otherwise it gets is not the main point to me. What matters is that there is this element of irrationality, the searching inside things that aren't logical or reasonable. It's a fact that we do things just because it seems right; financial analysis isn't even a consideration. Why do I do what I do? For the most part, for better or worse it has been for no real reason at all.

Passion.

Which explains *Leaving Venice*. The granular resynthesis of soprano melodies, the vocoded keyboard parts, the layers of polyrhythms. It's a dream sequence. It's a mystery novel, it's a black and white hand-held indie film, it's something I can't tell you about because it's not real; it is a fantasy of suggestion and imagination.

Her voice lingers, like the memories that float through the inner cinema of my mind as I stand on the platform watching the trains gliding by. I'm not listening to them, I have a different soundtrack in my mind. It's a mashup, a superimposed imagery upon reality that makes everything clearer somehow. Clarity of meaning. Rearrangement of context.

There is a border between reality – the known quantities and entities and expectancies – and the ethereal nothingness of the unexplored or unexplained. That's where I'm headed. I'm headed across that frontier. I'm waiting for the midnight express to Moscow. I want a new kind of clarification to those things that don't quite add up when I tap the numbers into my calculator app.

That is how it started. In a fleeting moment, standing on a platform somewhere. It was maybe 20 years later. And there was this flash of a moment in Venice that just flew by like a ghost train that doesn't need to stop at mortal stations anymore. It was a huge instance, in every extreme meaning of that oxymoron. Filled with the feelings of passion and mystery that must have been simmering on a low burner for all those years. Why then and more importantly why at all? I don't know. But the vibe, the feeling, the atmosphere, the sensuality, the overall sound came in on one big blast of air, like the sensation you get when the train roars out of the tunnel at speed and you're standing on the electric side of the yellow safety line. Pretty shocking and pretty arresting. I'm paying attention now, thank you very much.

This has happened to me before. Frequently. This is how it works for me at least. The big ideas, the big projects, the stuff that's going to be really worth it, come in one super nova of compacted energy with all the trimmings. It is as if it were an extremely compressed moment that needs to be expanded, stretched out, restored to its intended duration. Time compress Mahler's 7th so many times it plays back in less than one second. That's what I'm talking about.

So from that moment on, the work becomes unraveling the contents of this hyper-compacted vision, trying to understand what is really there, digging into the fragments and piecing it together.

Figuring out how to make each of those moments into a track or a scene or a movement gets all hung up in the little bits of exactitude that tangible work requires. Precision and fantasy are strange associates, indeed. But without a commitment to make it true to the vision, what's the point? The point is to try to realize the idea that has presented itself and to make absolutely sure I don't go off on some riff that leads nowhere.

So it is a struggle to make it good. To make it precise. To make it accurate. To dig in and really nail it.

I was using a studio that I had designed and built by hand, the first high definition surround sound studio in St. Louis.

I should mention that this was about 1998. That should say a lot. Although I didn't know it at the time, it was the end of an era, the end of the great period of 90's electronica and the work I was building was the last Deep House project that I did. As it turns out, this was the culmination of nearly 15 years of exploration into deeper and more remote regions of the world of experimental electronica. In retrospect it was the final statement that all those years of tracks led up to. But at the time, all I knew was I was trying to realize a vision of something that looked backward into memory with techniques and materials that were searching for the future.

Ending and starting.

Arriving and leaving.

Some affairs carry an edge that just doesn't ever go away. At some moment long after the kiss that turned out to be the last one, there is a moment when it has clearly ended. But the long fade never completely finishes. The audio never drops to a real zero. There is a thinly evaporating reverb tail that envelopes everything from that moment forward.

...

Ideas arrive as tightly compacted balls of energy. They bounce around the room and come to rest within the frame of our perception. *Our point of reference.* That's why I'm always looking, always working to expand my focal distance. I don't want to miss anything. I want to make sure my receptors are working, I want my range of awareness to be huge – as expansive and all embracing as it can possibly be.

Development is the way we uncover the full potential of ideas. It is the discernment of real significance and purpose, the revelation of tangible value and potential. Through the craft of discovery, the ideas of our raw inspiration become conscious, tangible concepts – complete in all dimensions and ready to become tangible works.

Discovery is the view expansive. It pierces the limitations of reference and reaches out to embrace the world, its communities, and its peoples. The craft of discovery is the search for new kinds of beauty, a richer spirit, a vision of something better.

It is our most intense idea, unpacked.

And it is driven by an intense passion to discover what tomorrow can be.

Third

Development

and the craft of resourcefulness

Seeing,
Seeing something out there,
A flash of an idea,
Highly compacted and brilliant,
It is more, much more.

Dig down, develop,
Expand,
Explore.
This is the spirit of expression, revealed.

Artifact

"I'm gonna pass" – Mr. Art Director, Leo Burnett, Chicago

I'm sure he doesn't remember me. And I don't remember his name. But I remember the conversation. He passed on my reel. But before he did, he had the decency to give me his feedback, however painful it was to receive at the time.

His perspective was that the production values in my reel were not at the level of a "final." He was right. I didn't have any finals on my reel because at that point I hadn't done any. I tried to explain that I had the skill and the experience if he'd give me a chance. But he was sticking to what he heard and that was as far as it was going to go.

That day I learned that a demo is never a "demo."

It is always the real thing.

And I learned that people in high places aren't likely to bet their careers and reputation on some kid they don't even know.

I understand that now.

Audiences and customers and investors are just the same. They don't care if you've got skills. All they care about is what they can see with their own two eyes.

No one is going to care that the reason your work is lame is because you couldn't afford the proper paint, didn't have time to have the piano tuned, or the digital converters were from 1984. It will be painfully obvious to everyone that it's just not happening.

Excuses just don't count.

Whatever you're showing has to totally work within the confines of available resources. Period.

Across the Frontier

"Roads? Where we're going, we don't need roads."
- Dr. Emmett Brown

Georgia O'Keefe and I have just crossed the border in a rented van with *Gringo* splashed across the side in bold fluorescent green letters. Well, actually it says "$19.95" on it. She needed to retrieve about a dozen paintings from her show at a museum.

I called ahead, reserved the truck. Everything sounded cool. But when we got to the rental counter the guy asked me again where we were headed.

"Over there," I said, vaguely pointing south.

"Well, we don't have any insurance for Mexico," he said.

Hmm. That just made things a lot more *interesting*. Sometimes the provisions and materials don't fit in the family sedan. A little cargo space is necessary. I had not choice but to go for it.

"Just don't tell me where you're going and you can have the van. People do it all the time…"

Yes, there are a lot of layers to this creativity thing.

…

The town where creativity lives sits on the border between the familiar and the unknown. And like every border town I've ever known it's a complex mix of intrigue, mystery, danger, and excitement. Here on the border, our ideas find new contexts and references, look into new faces, hear new languages.

Development is an expedition that begins in the familiar and ends somewhere out there, across the frontier, in a place no one has ever been before. Development is the exploration of possibility, it is the way ideas become expanded, extended, refined, and their full potential is discovered.

We fill the great microbus of discovery with tools, skills, a vision, supplies, a team of supporters and financial wizards, and head out into the open. There are no roads, no signposts, no bridges. It is a journey of pure experimentation, trial and error, and more than a few wrong turns and many mistakes.

But this is where the real potentials and possibilities are. Wide open space where there are no limits or pre-existing expectations. The craft of development is the system that sees beyond the constraints of conventional structure, and establishes the foundation for the nuts and bolts implementation of the idea. It is the way we establish the methods and procedures that will allow us to move into the implementation and completion, to actually make stuff happen.

That's why we're all here.

...

Development is the experimentation that leads to the most direct and original way to express the idea. The power of our creative vision is made useful and real through the experimentation – trial and error – the craft of development. It is the result of the application of time, effort, resources, and imagination in the pursuit of something entirely new.

Development is the search for the most effective form for an idea. The genre, structure, content, vocabulary – voice – that expresses the purpose and meaning most clearly and powerfully. Arriving at the physical form that will become the tangible statement of an idea is an activity that discovers potential and opportunities beyond the conventions of anything that already exists.

Experimentation is the search for the extremity of an idea, the idea expanded and extended, fully revealed.

It is the search for the new.

Originality is the result of new explorations and new materials. It is the result of crossing the line between what is commonly accepted as possible and seizing the impossible.

Originality is more than new or different, it is unique and without president. But it takes a powerful level of originality to turn the whole world towards a new direction.

Standard formulas and templates aren't going to get us where we need to go. Conventional thinking yields conventional results. That's not good enough.

The craft of development needs to embrace experimentation and exploration. Testing, research, and a willingness to try the improbable. Mistakes will be made, stuff will break. That's good. It takes some time to do this right, some time to cross enough borders to finally arrive at methods that actually work, that achieve the full vision.

This craft of development is critical and necessary. It is the means through which our ideas become real. It is through these real, tangible forms that the world confronts the import of our ideas.

…

The idea to write a multimedia opera emerged at the low point of my career when I had come to the realization that it was necessary to do something that would either raise my career to a sustainable level or end it completely. I was prepared to either succeed or fail, to either move forward or give up.

In terms of my creative work, it was the confrontation between a determined vision and the realities of circumstance. One or the other would prevail and I was ready to get on with it.

It was indeed a desperate and drastic time.

It was clear from the beginning that the main purpose of the work was to be a statement that was grand, profound, and innovative. It needed to be something that would unequivocally command attention; it had to be something that hadn't been done before in Chicago. I knew that was the only way to rebuild my career.

Fortunately, I had at least seen a map.

For ten years my day (and night) job was in symphony orchestra operations as the liaison between the grand ideas of the conductor and the harsh realities of the theatre production managers. Over hundreds of productions I learned what works and how to get professionals to work together to achieve excellence. I knew that if I could write the work, I could produce it.

The uncharted frontier that stretched out before me was the long and unknown development cycle of crafting my artistic vision into a tangible, performable piece of powerful music.

And it all began with the vision, the concept, and the underlying theme. For the work to be profound, I reasoned, it needed to touch upon something deeper than the traditional love themes of classic opera. Having grown up watching the horrors of the Vietnam War on my family's television, I have always thought that peace among the world's people should be the highest priority of our time. This work became my opportunity to implement that conviction.

I researched the events of peace movements in the American South, in the Troubles of Ireland, among the countries of the Middle East, and the confrontations resulting from occupations in the colonial era.

Over several years, the libretto evolved from a simple retelling of events to the stunningly direct and gripping excerpts of primary source material collected from the letters, speeches, and writings of over fifty people active in the non-violence movement.

As the libretto was evolving, I was writing the vocal lines and orchestrations to individual scenes that portrayed significant events such as the Freedom Summer of the American Civil Rights movement, Gandhi's attempt to quiet a rioting crowd in Calcutta, and life on Robbin Island in South Africa during the Apartheid era.

Simultaneously, I was sitting up nearly every night in front of the screen of my NeXT computer assembling and rendering the computer music files that would become the continuous sonic backdrop of the work.

The visuals were created at the very last minute and consisted of projected texts of quotations that gave additional depth and context to the scenes being portrayed on stage.

The work was premiered in 1994 at The Cindy Pritzker Auditorium in the Harold Washington Public Library, Chicago, Illinois. The development of the work had taken only two years but I knew it was not over. During the next eight years, the work went through three more significantly revised production versions including a series of performances in New York City with support from the National Endowment for the Arts.

Despite my sincerest intentions to place as much rationality as I can upon the future, a lot of the significant stuff that I've done has been the result of either desperation or necessity. But of those illogical acts of artistic intensity, I regret none of them. It seems, looking back, that the big works, and even the ones that didn't resonate significantly at the time, have all made a lasting impression on my practice and on people they have touched.

Years later, the stuff is still working.

So I jump in.

And logic gets pushed aside.

And the craft of development takes over. Stuff gets made. And in large or small ways, something changes. We are all lifted a little bit higher.

...

The craft of development is a commitment to push harder and further into the vast frontier of the unknown, the future.

The work that brings our ideas to the brink of reality is an expedition of discovery that begins in the familiar and sometimes dangerous frontier town at the edge of the wilderness. It requires us to collect our supplies, assemble a support team that has enough credibility that we can trust them with the life of the idea, and then we set out. Moving deeper and deeper into places never before seen, unknown even in the most sophisticated theory books, far beyond the conventional imagination.

The craft of development is a science lab where real objects coalesce and take form out of materials and imagination. But even more than that, it is an expedition of extreme potential, a journey into places never before imagined, to places where the outcome is entirely unknown. A series of adventures small, and sometimes very large, that bring us to a place that is the foundation of pure originality.

Raw Exploitation

Break it down, melt it, use it.

Where has my VGA monitor gone? Where have all those green screens gone?

Someplace like Asia.

The inspiring and sometimes shocking reality of living in a world that is both developed and developing simultaneously is that the objects of one world take on entirely new meanings in the other. The highly complex tools such as computers and machinery of my neighborhood are eventually discarded, rendered obsolete by newer and more developed versions, and they end up in the remote corners of the world, far from their original context. There, the original purpose and meaning is often absurdly useless and maybe even enigmatic – what's this thing do? Instead of seeing the object for its higher level purpose – a computer perhaps – it becomes simply a package of components, parts, metals, plastics. It becomes a small bundle of raw material.

That's where the Melter Dudes come in. They tear my old IBM green screen apart and melt down the boards, extracting the metals and selling them The alarming thing of course is that a good amount of toxic fumes and other bad stuff is released into the family home at the same time. And the cooking pot used to melt this stuff down is the same pot that dinner is prepared in. All very much not good.

...

I lived in Brooklyn for a short time with a family friend, my Fairy Godmother. She gave me shelter while I finished the production of my opera at a venue in Soho. It was the late 80s. Soho was different then – lofts and galleries and no shoe stores. It was on the edge, the fringe, as hard as it is to believe today. The Guggenheim had a space there where experimental works were shown. I saw my first Bill Viola there. His stuff blew me away.

It was a time and place where "new" was happening everywhere. But what was most exciting to me, an independent artist, was that it was all happening without big industrial-sized budgets. It was, arguably, the beginning of a collective understanding that great work can happen with the materials available; that it doesn't take huge uptown resources – venues and finances – to create something exciting and compelling. The materials themselves stop being a constraint and become the inspiration that propels innovation. The materials spark new insights and possibilities.

The craft of development is the way we approach the tools and materials. It is our ability to assess expanded visions of potential from within the borders of tangible assets – time and raw materials.

...

My dad, The Inventor, was an industrial engineer. When he wasn't dreaming up new mechanical objects to make daily life better – or at least different – his day job was obsessing over a piece of machinery that stretched the distance of a city block. He was in charge of an aluminum rolling mill. It was the biggest thing I'd ever seen. Needless to say, I grew up knowing how mechanical stuff worked; taking things apart was just something we did.

But the best part of this set of conditions was that the "surplus," the cast-off materials of construction at the plant, became the raw materials of my childhood. There was, for example, the time when a machine the size of a dump truck was delivered to the plant encased in a huge wooden crate. The weekend after the machine had been uncrated and installed on the mill floor, a lot of great lumber was left lying around out in the yard. That's where my tree house came from. Free materials, lots of free materials.

But the coolest residual benefit I gained from this situation was wire. It seems that in a place like this, where distance and size takes on an entirely new proportion, there were *a lot* of really long telephone lines. And when a telephone line had to be moved or repaired, the phone company guys would just yank out the old line, wad it up into a ball, and throw it off to the side before installing the new wires. It made a lot of sense to them, I'm sure.

Great – not to worry, we have people that will clean that up for you.

So I ended up with lots of phone wire that became the power grid of my world of experimentation in lighting effects and multiple speaker installations.

Of course, you see this coming. Fast forward to 1980s Soho and I'm checking out The Museum for African Art that was just up the street from the Guggenheim. In the shop I discovered beautiful woven baskets and bowls made from – telephone wire. This was actually a life changing moment for me, as simple and obvious as it seems today. Yes, that same striped, multicolored, 22 gauge wire that I had been the recipient of as a kid had been scavenged by weavers in South Africa as raw material for their work. The result was as beautiful as objects woven from plant fiber; perhaps even more beautiful because of the interesting patterns of colors that resulted from the consistent series of color-coding stripes on the wire.

Every object that exists is raw material for something beyond its intended purpose.

It is the fundamental need to create, to express a vision with whatever materials are at hand. Whether it's in the villages or the townships of Jo-berg, or the concrete neighborhoods of a first world city, or in any large or small corner of the vast community we all share, there are materials waiting to be used, waiting to become the source – the raw resources of our creative work Third world, second world, first world, tenth world, it is fundamentally the same. A vision needs to be implemented – and it is through our ingenuity and inventiveness and sheer determination that we can find a way to express it with the resources present here and now.

These women, for whom weaving was their heart, soul, and very livelihood, looked around and got inventive. They abandoned the limitation of preconceptions of material. No traditional materials were available but the discovery and manipulation of new methods and new techniques worked just fine, thank you.

Originally, these wire baskets were woven from truly surplus wire obtained the same way my dad and I got it. The stuff was simply left behind, discarded by the installers who couldn't be bothered with cleaning up that old useless stuff. No problem. It was literally like pulling something out of the dumpster, free for the taking.

...

Soho is different now. It is an entirely different place from the one that inspired me to see past the surface of materials. The Guggenheim Soho where I was so completely blown away by Bill Viola's "Fire, Water, Breath" closed in 2001. Its first floor space was reborn as a Prada shoe store.

The Museum for African Art closed its Soho location and is looking for funding to build a new space on East 110th – in a part of the city with an entirely different heritage and context.

The wire baskets have become commercialized and the materials are no longer scavenged or stolen. With the high cash value of metal now, especially the copper used in telecommunication wire, the weavers compete with the Melter Dudes for raw material. Weaving has had to adapt and change from a grass-roots, gorilla-style independent artisan model to a more stable cottage industry with established sources of raw materials and worldwide distribution.

As a result, the weavers have lost the leading edge of recycled art to objects made from soda cans – a practice begun by West African children making their own toys from whatever they could find.

And like the jazz loft scene, the independent artist collectives, and the sweatshops that preceded them, Soho itself has been again completely repurposed. Here, as in countless other neighborhoods, the buildings and the environment have always been simply raw material to be exploited and recycled for new purposes of the moment. A constantly changing application of content, redesigned and realigned to a vision that is ever moving forward, reaching out, looking for something new. The buildings, the neighborhood, the recycled computer monitors, the telephone wire, and the shipping crate, are in reality the raw material waiting to be exploited by a craft of development that sees the potential beyond the surface.

It was as I stood there that day in the museum, looking at those wire objects for the first time, that my perception of material and resource was recalibrated. The material that becomes the content and form of our vision is no longer simply items off the shelf, ordered from a catalog to be used for a preconceived purpose. The key to real creative work is seeing material as a collection of potential that is not predetermined. I understood for the first time that real creative work is the result of seeing the application of resources in a way that no one has ever seen them before.

Discovery is not only the way we develop our methods and establish our procedures, it is most significantly our ability to envision the implementation and content of something in a way that no one has ever conceived of it before.

The result of artistic creation has nothing to do with the high price of raw materials and everything to do with finding ways to use the materials at hand in the most expressive way possible.

Wire *is* in fact simply a medium of expression – As it is lying there on the rolling mill floor in a jumbled heap it is in fact an object of high energy, extreme potential, raw material waiting to be exploited. But that's precisely the point. It is there waiting for someone to come along with the ability to perceive its potential.

The craft of development implements our ability to discover the unknown, the unforeseen, the new and unexpected; to transport us to a place no one has ever been before with tools that no one has ever contemplated using in ways that have never been tested. It is extreme experimentation, discovery, it is the way the unknown becomes known.

...

The real meaning of raw is this ability to de-couple the component parts of something from its initial intended concept or purpose. It is the ability to see potential embedded within the materials divorced from their connection or association with other component parts. And even more significantly, it is the ability to envision new ways these isolated elements can be useful to meet needs that have nothing to do with the purpose or intent of the original object, work, or idea.

The craft of development is the envisioning of the presence of opportunity, the ability to see a realization of vision in the often disparate concepts of raw material.

It is, in every direction, the exploitation of the true meaning of raw.

The Computer and the Hammer

The instruments of expression, the weapons of persuasion – tools blunt and sharp.

Thor and The Persuader.
    Hammers have a lot of personality. Different weights, sizes, and shapes according to the purpose.
    The Persuader is a 20-pound sledgehammer. I bought it back in '85 when I first moved to Wisconsin. Together with a wedge, I used it to split wood for my fireplace. Since then, I've used it to tear down walls when necessary and to generally convince things to go some place they really didn't want to go.
    I've had Thor since 1977. It's small, massive, and looks prehistoric. Back then I had a '65 MGB with real knock-off wire wheels. There were two of them in the boot. So when I had to sell the car I decided to keep one of the hammers for myself.
    And then there's the computers. A long lineage of hardware that I'm far too attached to; we just spent way too many hours together for me to send them off to the recyclers now. There's my crazy teal-colored SGI Octane, my NeXT slab that I spent almost every night with for over a year writing the opera, a Mac Plus fully loaded with

4MB of RAM that was the first computer I had that could do music notation, and my workhorse Pismo laptop upgraded with an aftermarket CPU to a 900 MHz G3. The overclocking finally imploded and it won't run anymore. I like to think he's gone back to hangin' at the beach.

...

Tools blunt or sharp.

Tools are the means of expressing our ideas, of communicating our inspiration. They extend our reach, multiply our force, amplify the volume of our content. Tools allow us to implement the project in ways that we couldn't on our own. Tools are the means through which the work is realized.

Tools are often essential to achieve the purpose. So choose something powerful. Limitations stink. Choose something highly refined. Refinement is about excellence and appropriateness. It is about being perfectly suited to the task.

Something that works every time.

Something like a hammer, perhaps.

...

How often, especially at the beginning, did I just use whatever was available? Reached down and grabbed whatever tool was lying there? Especially in regard to highly expensive hardware for many years I could afford only one tool. And unavoidably that one tool pretty much defined my capabilities. I had grown tired of the limitations of the low-budget tools I used. I had grown tired of potential clients telling me that some of the work was lame when I knew it was the package, the surface, the execution – and not the idea, itself – I realized the work wasn't good enough. It was frustrating to know that the music I was composing was being limited by the low-quality execution of the tools I had available.

So I decided to go after the best tool out there. And in this particular story of tools blunt and sharp, the outcome was complicated and emotional. Sort of like a love story.

I came within moments of betting everything on a very shiny Fairlight CMI Series IIx sitting in the glass-walled super-room of Gand Music and Sound. I saw this very expensive and high-profile instrument as a way to raise the level of my execution to the highest standard of the day. And as a result I also thought it would attract more clients to my music production company. In Chicago at the time, there was only one other commercial producer who had one.

I was pretty sure that being able to flash around that kind of bling would attract some attention. But would it attract clients? Would it pay for itself? There was no way to know the answer to those questions without taking the plunge. And I balked.

At the time, the Fairlight CMI was the highest quality electronic musical instrument available. There really wasn't any other device that could do what it did in a way that was as musical and realistic. Nothing could substitute for the Fairlight. On that basis, I blew it.

Tools are either blunt or sharp. It's easy to fall in love with either kind. But it's the sharp ones that can really hurt when they break or turn out not to deliver on the promise of their exactitude.

Did I make the right decision?

Perhaps those monthly payments would have been just a little more tangible incentive for me to get out there and make more contacts, find more clients – do even better work. Maybe it would have been the motivation that would have kicked my little operation up to the next level. All that would have been a genuinely good outcome.

But what if the clients didn't materialize? Ugly.

To this day, I wasn't sure if compromising on an alternative product was brilliant or stupid. So I cracked open the history books:

It turns out, predicting the future isn't so easy – who knew? Fairlight went bankrupt in late 1988 and the last IIx was sold through Gand Music and Sound. Fairlight didn't or couldn't pay Gand the sales commission. So Gand sued Fairlight. But Gand never received the settlement because Fairlight went bankrupt a few days later.

Was this particular IIx the one in the history books? Based on the dates and the fact that Gand told me it was the last IIx available, I'm pretty sure it was. Interesting.

In the end, I would have been the last person on Earth to purchase an extremely expensive dinosaur. Lovely, beautiful, charming, but totally obsolete within a matter of months.

So what's the take away on all that? The biggest hang-up to this entire exercise in speculation is the fact that I was stretching everything to afford it. No matter how incredible that piece of gear was the burden of financial risk took all the benefits down.

Let's add in a small bit of economic context: Black Monday. I distinctly remember October 19, 1987. My partner and I were out making sales calls. Sitting in the car with the radio on, news of the crash hit me like a wave of ice cold water. I knew at that moment business would pull inward, budgets would shrink, and work would dry up. In the months following, the decline in the level of corporate spending for advertising was huge. It took years for the ad industry to regain pre-Black-Monday levels. By mid-1988, things were really not looking all that much better for us. We survived between gigs because we were young, willing to eat cheap food, and our fixed costs were essentially zero – no kids, no flashy cars, nada.

Feeling like a fool for being the last one to the Fairlight party would have been bad enough, but having the monthly payments pull down the whole operation would have been far more than embarrassing.

It would have been purely stupid.

...

A friend runs a sound company providing racks and stacks for weddings and corporate. It's very hard work. Heavy schlepping and infinitesimal profit margin. Does anyone really want to pay for sound? Isn't that, like free, with the band or whatever?

One time we were talking. He had just bought about 5 grand worth of JBL cabinets. Standing there looking at the guy it was hard for me to image he could put that kind of change together. So I asked him if there could have been a cheaper alternative.

Suddenly, he launches into a litany of all the lame gear he'd bought in his time and how it had messed with his life in a thousand different ways when it fell apart at the gig. The fact is, gear that's built cheaply is just fine if you're not pushing it. But take it on the road, throw it into a van three or more nights a week for a while and it's not going to be your friend for life. In fact it will stab you in the back at the worst possible time.

...

Stuff breaks.

Sometimes on purpose.

Circuit Bending? Awesome. It's a lot easier to rationalize the downside of crossing wires when it's a $15 Furby. I think this has taught all of us a number of important lessons.

First, being willing and financially able to push something to the point of breaking can have significantly exciting results. Risking loosing something is no reason to be shy with the tool. If you're not willing to break it, you shouldn't be using it.

Starting with some existing circuitry can drastically shorten the development time. Find something that sort of does the job, and Frankenstein it.

But sometimes there's just nothing on the shelf that'll do the job. Well, that's when it's time to roll your own, my friend.

Frankly, it's getting pretty obvious that it takes new tools to create new work. And I'm not just talking search engines or software apps. When industrial-grade science – materials and processes – gets applied to food, sculpture, amplification, construction, or fabrics, exciting new stuff happens. It's all about devising an original tool to do something that has never been done before.

And it doesn't have to be complicated. I spent one summer of my college career making round wire into flat wire. It was an absurdly simple machine. A spool of round brass wire on the left and a collection roller on the right. In the middle was a very small pair of rollers and a motor. The wire fed from the left to the right and was flattened by the rollers. Simple. But it was the foundation of a multimillion-dollar business making something we all use every day. A very small piece of that flat wire acts as a type of staple to hold the bristles into their holes on the head of the toothbrush. Check it out next time you've got a moment in the morning. That little piece of metal jammed down in the hole keeps the bristles from pulling out.

Get the tools right, and the tools will generate work that is wildly unique, exciting, and unprecedented.

It used to take industrial budgets to do something like that. But building your own original tools, or repurposing tools to functions in ways that have never been tried before, is a lot easier now. All of this is as close as the nearest laptop, the surplus store, or home improvement center. Got PVC?

...

In the end, it comes down to the recognition that achieving the inspiration, communicating the vision, sharing the purpose is what really counts. And tools help make that happen. Power tools, vintage gear, original stuff, they all extend our capabilities or lead us into worlds of entirely new opportunities, new possibilities.

So push stuff hard, find out just how much pressure can be applied before something shatters. It takes a few attempts to learn when to back off. It's a highly nuanced balance between practicality and extremity; a realistic mediation between affordability and betting the farm.

Standing on the creative edge, holding that line between free falling and not, can be pretty scary. A strong rope and a carabiner or two just might make all the difference.

The right tools give us leverage. Push them hard, apply some pressure and some heat, really lean into it. They give us a little bit of certainty that it is actually possible to do this crazy stuff – that these ideas might actually work.

Fourth

---

*Implementation
and the craft of momentum*

*Ideas have the power to inspire and change.
They take shape in ways that reach out and grab us,
In a form we can hold.
Words, songs, colors, constructions.
The power of ideas is the capacity to touch the heart,
To show us a better way.*

Ideas move us with the power of a vision made real.

Artifact

From a recent online auction site:
Speak & Spell Vintage 1980s Electronic Educational
Learning Game: $13.50
Speak and Spell Circuit Bent: $229.00

There are no rules, no conventions, no givens – anymore.

Implementation is about accepting that nothing is off limits, nothing is sacred. There is nothing that is off the table, ever.

No matter what venue the work lands in, no matter where the idea is coming from or the trajectory that lies ahead, accept no boundaries, don't get sucked into accepting anything as inherently necessary. And there is nothing that is absolutely essential, either.

There are no established norms anymore. The world has changed and the way stuff gets accomplished now has far more to do with seeing the potential of available resources than following the established techniques of the past.

Throw away all preconceptions of right and wrong implementation, leave every notion of established practice where it belongs, in the desk drawer with the dictionaries and phone books. It's all absurdly irrelevant now.

We need to crack open the box, grab some wire, and make something entirely new and unexpected happen, right now.

Back in 1966 when Reed Ghazala pulled open his metal desk drawer and accidentally shorted his toy transistor amplifier, a stream of sound never before heard poured from the speaker.

Cool.

Ghazala's genius was that he recognized the potential of the accident and went on to develop the practice he eventually called circuit bending – the spontaneous manipulation of existing low-voltage electronic toys and instruments for the purpose of generating unique and original sounds.

Used Furby?

Cute maybe, but I'm thinking not. It's been done way too many times already.

No matter what the form the idea ultimately will take, the implementation has to be unique and individual. Conventional ways lead to established results. There are no prizes for being second, third, or last to the party anymore.

The only thing that matters now is being first.

So as we raise the work into the clear cold light of the real world, this is the craft of implementation:

The necessary finding of a creative action, an implementation, that's never before been contemplated. And discovering the means to achieve it.

It's About Power Really

And the boldness to actually use it.

I'm serious.

The reason we're doing all this hard work is to find a way to express an idea with such intensity that it causes a seriously large impact. Stuff needs to change; we need to find some real solutions to the hard problems that confront us. We need some hard-core creative work that can go out there and make a real difference – here and now.

Whether the form is a novel or short story, a symphony or a duet, it doesn't matter in the least if the function, the intent, is communicated in a way that is compelling and effective. Creativity is not powerful or meaningful just because it comes packaged in a large and impressive box. There are plenty of blatantly stupid and useless symphonies, operas, novels, major films. Works that touch us most deeply, that stick with us the longest, are not simply the biggest, fastest, loudest, or brightest things we have ever seen. The stuff that really slams us, picks us up and heads us in a new direction, are statements that are powerful because they are the most directly expressive representations of a highly compelling concept.

...

When I get wrapped up in the possibility of composing something for a symphony orchestra, the possibilities of implementation carry me away – I can't resist imagining the incredible array of sounds and textures. But that's backwards thinking: I'm composing from the standpoint of the implementation, rather than building from the foundation of the concept, purpose, or idea. And it completely ignores the fact that it's totally ridiculous for me to even contemplate a project of that scope under my current circumstances. My life is way too fragmented to be able to focus on something that long-range.

Not to mention, there's no symphony orchestra waiting to play the thing, either.

The fact is, the world really doesn't need another symphony. What it needs is a new idea, a better vision of what life could be. That, we need. If that vision can be communicated best through the form of a symphony, then it is exactly what we need. But just another orchestra piece, sitting in the drawer? No, that's not the objective.

The point is to implement ideas that are powerful enough to inspire change and make everything it touches, better.

The craft of implementation is where we dig down to the core, the foundation of what you're really trying to accomplish – what is really worth saying – and then find a way to say it in the most compelling way possible.

The craft of implementation seizes the depth and richness of the idea – the breadth and potential generated by the development cycle – and makes the idea into something that reaches out and touches us all.

The fundamental basis of any work is an abstract vision, an idea or statement that needs to be expressed. It is this vision, this statement, not the materials that is the purpose of the work. Implementation is not a commitment to specific materials and form. The materials serve the vision and the message. The work is not about the materials; it's not even about the content, either.

Use form. Don't let form dictate the statement. Form is the container for expression; expression does not conform to structure.

…

Concepts need to be separated from their form, their structure.

What really guides the determination of the form, the decision of materials and content, the shape of the work, is the necessity of precision and directness.

It's a demand in two parts: Clarity of expression and the immediacy of clear communication. The implementation – the words, chords, melodies, moves, colors, shapes – needs to be precise enough that the critical elements of the concept are expressed. And it needs to be structured to communicate within the expectations of the intended audience and users.

It's a balance. The goal is to find a way for something exceptional to be achieved with the resources available. Going into a project with preconceived expectations of form drastically reduces the options for finding a balance between expression and communication.

Finding a balance means keeping the concept, the idea, the statement in the foreground, not the materials. The idea can be communicated in a variety of media – some are more practical and achievable than others under the circumstances of available resources.

There are many, many ways to express an idea. An idea can be expressed in an infinite number of different forms. Some are more direct and effective than others.

The media is the voice, not the message.

Keep the focus on the power of intent and hold implementation in service to the message.

…

Ideas are powerful, they energize and inspire. They travel at light speed and reach far beyond borders.

Ideas show us a new way of looking at our world.

They give us a new vision.

A vision that rises above the limits of brick and mortar thinking.

A vision of change that's both personal and universal.

Ideas work. Ideas have impact.

Ideas are the catalyst and the energy that motivates and impels us all forward.

Ideas touch us all, embrace us all.

Ideas reach out and lift us all higher. Together.

That's why all this is so important.

Ideas have great power when expressed in their most direct form. The intensity of creative ideas can change us for the better.

Micromanagement

It's all those little things in life that really matter.

Sweat the details.

Or maybe it's simply refining, or editing, or revising, or being obsessive, or being thorough – exhaustive, even. Or maybe it's simply just not "settling," or compromising the vision, or being talked out of the right way to do it.

It's all about holding on against the pull of practicality and bravely ignoring reality. It's the total opposite of giving up.

It's simply wanting the work to be perfect.

Is that asking too much?

Getting there is more than just not caving in whenever the producer says, "No one will ever notice that in the mix." It's not going along when someone offers you a substitute fabric that costs half as much as the real stuff and is *almost as good.* Man, it hurts just thinking about wearing that polyester stuff, doesn't it?

We all know where this is going.

But what makes that compromise so obviously stupid? Details. The form and structure of the work on a micro scale.

For argument's sake, let's consider my first grand piano – a Kimball. It didn't *look* all that different from the Steinway or Yamaha that I really wanted but couldn't afford. Except, from the very first note it was clear that it didn't play like one of those instruments. No tone, no expression, and no touch. It seemed like none of the details were happening. Nothing was really excellent. Maybe it was the materials or the methods. I can't say for sure but I suspect it was about the vision, or lack of it. Thinking it's Ok to compromise on the resources and materials because "no one will ever notice" just never ends well. By now we all should know, *everyone* is noticing.

Form has a lot to do with holding implementation on course, it has a lot to do with keeping the focus, getting the work finished, having it fulfill the intended purpose and make a strong and clear statement.

It's structure on two levels. Macro- and Micro-structure: the form IN and the form OF the work. The cool colors and shapes draw you in and then the micros take over and deliver the message.

Like the zoom tool in software the structural considerations within the work are at every point between 99.999% and 0.001%. We're talking infinitely variable levels of detail between the individual digital samples and the relationship between the chorus and the verse; the individual hair lines of the brush stroke to the overall shapes and colors of each component of the design.

While boarding a plane today, I noticed the individual latches that held the flight attendant's cabinet doors closed – surprisingly substantial examples of finely machined metalwork. They made me realize that as I'm sitting here in the cabin, all the details that I can see combine into an impression that everything about this machine is of the highest quality. Subconsciously, if not rationally, the overall impression is that this flying machine is going to hang together long enough to get me back to solid ground. And perhaps that's also why it's slightly disturbing when my seatback doesn't work or the tray table won't stow properly. I'm worried, a little, that maybe there's a few other, perhaps more critical things, that aren't exactly just right.

How easy would it have been to say, well, those cabinets don't make the plane fly, we could save something there. Maybe put in cheaper seats, make everything out of plastic. We could start to save some serious budget there. Pretty soon, we're walking onto some kind of Kimball with wings.

Scary.

Take a close look at the really great products, the really successful ads, the really innovative garments, the really landmark films. Get your zoom tool out and take a very, very close look. Put on those headphones and really pay attention. Freeze a lot of frames of video. You will see it. In the great works, impeccable details are literally everywhere.

...

If macro-structure is the roadmap, micro-structure is the white line on the edge of the road. It's there to keep us from falling off the edge and to give us something to focus on so we keep going in the right direction. The white line is a theme, a riff maybe, that keeps the groove going. It's the bass line of *In a Godda Da Vida*, or *Satisfaction*, it's the four-note opening of Beethoven's 5th Symphony. That white line keeps me in the lane and knockin' back those miles. With a really great theme, I'm a long way down the road towards having a great piece of music; with some really great images, I'm a long way towards a great looking film. It's far easier to fill those blank pages when there's a great story to tell. The micro-structure provides the framework from moment to moment, measure to measure, sentence to sentence, image to image, component to component.

In a very molecular way, the elements at the micro level float in space waiting to be connected together and given meaning and context through their association, their inter-relationships. There is an interchange of dialogue, the intercut of wide shots and close-ups, themes bump against each other and react. Dialogues are not two part monologues – conversations happen. Responses are triggered, actions are provoked. Tension, harmony, consonance, dissonance, logic confronts chaos, and darkness is illuminated.

Particles are smashed, neutrons are rearranged, concepts collide.

Energy is created.

...

And then there's this little thing called excellence. Everywhere. That's all.

Is perfection possible, ever? No one I know thinks so. It's a moving target. Get close, and the standard moves higher. In the physics of creativity, perfection is the speed of light, the closer you get to attaining it, the hard and harder it is to actually get there.

However unattainable, the pursuit of excellence and perfection is essential. Why? Because, the strength of communication relies on the *quality* of the work. The stronger the execution, the stronger the communication.

High quality expressivity results in statements that are compelling and engaging. The connection with the audience and the user makes an impact that is significant and lasting.

Excellence is the source of longevity. Ideas that stand the test of time, that become timeless or recalibrate everything around them, rise above the noise floor of everything else that is going on and command attention. They stand out because they are powerful and it is the energy, the intensity, instilled in the work through a dedication to excellence that generates the power of extraordinary impact and engagement.

Ideas need to connect, they need to grab attention and stick. Excellence powerfully arrests attention and forges a lasting engagement. As illusive and unattainable ultimate excellence or perfection is, the pursuit of it causes us to instill the work with an extraordinary level of energy and detail. It has the grit of a deeper humanity embedded within its very fiber. The whole thing is rocking and moving in sync like one body on the dance floor. And you know how exciting that is.

Sweat the details, chase perfection, charge every particle with the intensity of a higher vision, and the work will be infused with the power of excellence.

And it will be amazing.

It will rock.

Action

The idea is expressed THROUGH the work, so do something, already.

Like I really need to say it.

Doing good work, doing creative work is about *doing* stuff.

Stuff needs to get made.

Ideas alone? That's only half way. Without a tangible expression, they are just ideas, floating around in our imagination and never touching ground. That's not enough.

I'm talking about sitting down and actually sewing that new jacket design, or writing the poem, or composing a piano sonata, or writing some code, or choreographing a dance piece.

We need to make all those great ideas into something real, to bring them out into the light of day.

But there's a lot more to it than just building something.

It seems like the work is all about the practical application. It's a story, a song, a product. But what makes our work truly great is not its functionality alone. Great works express their underlying ideas through the medium of their form. There are two simultaneous layers of purpose going on at the same time: the function, and the meaning.

The only thing that really matters, the reason the work exists at all, is to communicate the underlying idea.

The work gives us a way to understand the idea, to make it our own, to adopt and implement it, and ultimately to incorporate it into our collective social and cultural consciousness.

Consequently, the work needs to communicate the idea as accurately and thoroughly as possible so it has a chance of succeeding – a chance of grabbing our collective attention long enough for us to grasp it and make it a part of ourselves.

Making stuff requires an ability to execute the craft well enough that the work delivers a compelling representation of its underlying idea.

The work tells us the story.

And the work communicates the idea.

…

Call it method.

The *way* we work makes a huge difference. It's a system, a framework, a structure.

Look up "schedule" in the dictionary and that's probably it. But I can't face it. That's way too rigid for my version of reality. I've never been able to stick to anything that rigorously. Life is just too variable for that. I wish I could work for four hours each morning. But that's never happened for me and probably never will.

Method is the situation we set up for ourselves that allows us to do some work. It's how we grapple with the issues of time and funding. It's what we absolutely need in terms of place and environment that allows us to do our best work.

Basically, it's enormous.

This is some of the most challenging and frustrating stuff to deal with that there is. But finding even a degree of success at any of it is crucial to creative survival.

Somehow enough time to do the best work has to materialize. And it needs to happen in a place where it's possible to actually focus on the project with enough intensity for it to actually get done.

Space, time, resources all need to come together.

There's some really serious stuff in the balance. Like life and jobs and family and friendships and physical health and mental stability.

So, be very careful.

Finding your work time and workspace doesn't just happen. It has to be carved out from other competing demands.

Very early on, it was clear to me that I wouldn't be able to keep at this work if I didn't develop a method that fit within my unique personal situation. By finding time within the cracks of a demanding work schedule and family responsibilities I was able to refine and master a systematic method of working that made it possible for me to keep going.

In my experience, method has been the single most important element in my ability to do the work that I have done. Without a conscious effort to evaluate my specific needs and to solve the conflicts that existed, nothing much would ever have seen the light of day.

The answers that worked for me were unique and site specific. Will they work for you? Maybe.

I always have more than one project going. For me, having a number of works in the pipeline keeps the momentum up. When something starts to get a little stale, I move to another thing, come back later. Nearly all of my composition students have more than one project cooking at the same time, too.

Three of my friends wrote their dissertations at coffee shops. A bass player friend of mine told me that he really needed to have the noise and activity around. He has a beautiful original craftsman-style home on the campus of a local divinity school but he said the silence in his home office was too intimidating and distracting – sort of like a real-world representation of the blank page staring him in the face.

Since becoming a "professional" – meaning actually earning money doing this stuff – I've worked just about anywhere I could. I now live in a house with twenty rooms and I have a choice of several workspaces. But it wasn't always this way, far from it. For the record here's an accounting, in chronological order, of my workspaces: my parent's living room, my boss's office in Orchestra Hall, nowhere, the bedroom my wife and I didn't use because we slept on a sofa bed in the living room so we could have a studio, our family room, a bedroom closet, our kitchen closet (seriously), our basement #2, the dining room, my in-law's basement, our basement #3, our breezeway. This book has been written in countless places with just my laptop wherever I can grab a moment to work – coffee shops, the snack bar at the college where I teach, in airports, and in the back rows of planes.

I did what I had to do. Some of the situations were better than others. Some weren't so bad, others barely worked at all. That's how I ended up in the kitchen closet. That's how I ended up practicing at 5:00 am.

Was that fun? Of course not.

Did it work?

Barely. But stuff got done; it was the only thing I could do at the time.

It had come down to that or nothing. And for some reason I just wasn't willing to accept nothing.

So I'll work anywhere, anytime I can. I'll grab it or steal it.

But somehow I'm going to do it.

...

There's a lot of things that will try to intimidate us. Try to put obstacles in front of our desire to do what we deeply cherish. Procrastination, discouragement, low self-esteem, personal conflicts. These things hit all of us at various times. They make it hard to have the openness and transparency that is necessary to fulfill the work. And when we feel that way, it seems like trying to be creative is the last thing we can face.

All of this comes down to the way we approach the work, the way we grapple with the tasks that need to get done.

Methods need to be effective. There is nothing in the realm of creative work that is more essential. The ability to actually execute an idea is the very necessity of bringing ideas into the real world where they can reach out and touch us, raise us up. It's that critical.

It's a dirty word, but I don't know any other way to accomplish things with any kind of consistency:

Discipline.

Sorry, but it helps.

Fifth

Completion

and the craft of determination

A river flows, the wind carries sound across a lake,
There is an energy,
An intensity in the power of ideas.
It is the work of lifetimes,
It is the work of this moment.

It is complete.
And the exploration begins
Anew.

Artifact

"Go ahead and jump." - *Eddie Van Halen*

I'm floating in a liquid iceberg. The waves shove me around, hold me up, suspended in weightlessness.

Lake Michigan; I love it. It's the one thing that's remained a constant throughout my whole life.

But that first plunge?

It always takes my breath away.

But I do it, anyway. Because no matter how shocking that first moment is, the rest is pure free fall.

Vivid. Sustaining.

…

There are days when it seems like everything in the world is a test. It measures our endurance, holds up our resolve to the piercing light of reality and gives it a good sharp poke.

Each morning, or whenever circumstances remind us just how cold the water is or how unforgiving reality can be, it is going to be tempting to turn aside and let the idea "just float away."

We need a spark, a point of departure. Something that pushes us across the threshold that separates in and out – something that shores up our endurance, day after day, moment upon moment. Something that keeps us there, working, undeterred and undistracted.

The fuel, the horsepower that keeps it all moving:

The shear weightlessness of floating in the waves.

Cue the Oberheim riff – pass on the hair.

Speed Bumps

The road to great work is littered with the obstacles of our own uncertainty.

Head games bad.

The biggest speed bump on the road to doing the work – for me and a lot of people that I know – is always the mental game: those little voices that carry on all manner of conflicting and confusing conversations in the dark recesses of underlying uncertainty.

There are all kinds of ways they slowly erode enthusiasm. And ultimately even money doesn't help.

The pain of just plain getting worn down; too many rewrites, too many revisions and too much conflicting input can far too easily come together and take the whole thing south.

There was a media producer in Milwaukee that I really wanted to work with. He got decent projects and his company had a cool vibe. Finally, after a couple of years he asked me to do a track. *On spec.*

Ok. I'll do that. Maybe I shouldn't but I will if I have the time and the project seems to have enough viability. And this one did. It was a national client. So I made a really cool, innovative track incorporating extensive use of sampling which was very new and hip at the time; it was 1989. He sends it back, with cryptic comments about how it needs more beat. So I make a couple more versions with harder, louder beats. All rejected with almost nonexistent guidance from the client about what should be changed.

It was a study in loosing traction and driving in circles; energy was applied but there was never any acceleration. I pondered what went wrong for a long time. Maybe there was too much baggage, too much unnecessary complexity, too much infrastructure, too many undeveloped relationships, too many missed connections.

After several tries we both just gave up. Way too vague; it just drained every last drop of inspiration out of the project.

In the end, it was pretty obvious no one had a clear idea of what the client wanted. It was basically a "fishing expedition." A real world version of hide and seek: "we'll know what we want when we see it." On spec, that is to say on someone else's money.

Holy guacamole. Let me out of that one.

But it happens all the time. I've watched myself and others flail around, trying all kinds of things and then *erasing or deleting it.*

Over the past decade or longer, I've watched a lot of people make beats. Some were really slammin'; a lot of them were not. It was an opportunity to observe craft from hundreds of different perspectives. And it showed me how much the success of the project depended on the method and craft of execution. The success of making beats is no different from any other creative work. It needs to be deliberate and thoroughly conscious.

I observed that the methods that resulted in really cool beats were organized, deliberate and thoroughly in touch with the vocabulary and purpose of the work.

The people that made really outstanding beats were intuitively and consciously in tune with the genre, they were knowledgeable of the scene, they were players in it, and constantly in touch with what was happening at every moment. Many were surprisingly well versed in the historical background of what they were doing, too. In short they lived and breathed this stuff and making beats was a natural, cognized extension of their engagement with life. There was no uncertainty and no questioning whether a track was cool or not. The craft of laying down tracks was meticulous, inspired, and coldly professional. Lay down a part, if it's cool then move on; if not, delete it and do it again. No hand wringing, no questioning, no problem.

But it didn't go down so well for a lot of other people. For them, it was one big mystery. And that was the part I just couldn't understand at first. I'd sit there and hear them make a cool track and then the next minute it had disappeared and something lame was happening. They would invariably delete the good stuff and keep the junk. Over and over.

Why, how?

There was no real idea there. Nothing. Nada.

They were just pushing buttons with no purpose, no knowledge, and no vision. It was just a mechanical exercise that had nothing to do with the functionality of the project.

They wanted very badly to make a beat, but they had nothing to go on, no knowledge of the style, no familiarity with how the beat would be used, not a clue about the expectations of the scene, and not even a concept of what a beat is trying to express or communicate.

They had absolutely no idea what a good beat sounded like. And they unfailingly missed it even when they randomly landed on something cool. They couldn't recognize a happenin' beat if it walked up and offered them a contract.

It's no wonder they couldn't differentiate between something cool and something stupid – it's impossible because there was nothing to measure the track against other than a personal judgment that has no basis in anything at all. It was simply an aimless attempt to find something they *liked*.

Subjectivity anyone? Sorry, but I just don't have time for it.

The biggest liability of relying on subjective, gut-level methods of evaluation – deciding whether content is cool or not based solely on how it hits us in the flash of the moment – is that stuff that is ordinary, expected, common, hackneyed is going to seem the most familiar and therefore the most subjectively "cool." It's cool because we've heard it before. Sometimes quite literally, we've subconsciously ripped it off. But we like it because in that brief moment it sounds just like everything else that's going on around us – it fits in, it blends, it fulfills a common expectation of coolness. And we're like, yeah, that rocks.

But it doesn't. Ultimately, it's boring. We've heard it all before. And it's not going anywhere.

Slow down a millisecond or two, hold on to a clear measure of the purpose of the content and stay in touch with the vision of our unique identity and the habitual struggle to generate excellent content will have a foundation based on something a lot more certain than "I like it." Or not.

The other thing that's happening is that judgments made with no conscious awareness of the actual *purpose* of the track make it completely impossible to arrive at a decision with any level of conviction. There's nothing to base a rational evaluation upon and we know it and it freaks us out. It pushes us into irrationality and we just pass on every single idea that comes our way, over and over again. We get into a mode of adamantly avoiding something that might end up being lame in the future – by nixing everything. And we end up with nothing.

It's a waste of time. And it's worse than that because good ideas get stomped on. Some great ideas just never see the light of day.

The craft of creativity is an expression of a broad range of knowledge and insight, cognitive order, purpose, and the ability to remain focused on the functionality of the project.

…

Roadblocks. There are a lot of things that will try to intimidate us, try to put obstacles in front of our desire to do the work we deeply cherish.

There's nothing that pulls down a project faster than the feeling of incompetence. That fragile little place between seeing things realistically and becoming consumed with the suspicion that one has completely "lost it" is about the most dangerous place I know. And I used to fall in there all the time.

When that happens, it's basically all over.

Comparisons. They're even worse. They start out sounding like an attempt to rationally figure out how to get good, get better at what we do. It begins by thinking about how amazing someone else is and wanting to know how they got that good. Then it heads south. So-and-so is awesome; I'm not. She's just so amazingly talented; I'm not. And it's not very long and I'm falling through space and never hitting bottom. Didn't my mom tell me that there's always going to be someone richer, taller, skinnier, cooler? Yes, I know.

Completely irrational, and yet entirely destabilizing.

Digging out of that deep dark place always takes an enormous amount of effort.

It takes help. Friends and family, anyone who supports us and our work, who is willing to offer even a fragment of encouragement or assistance can begin to turn this kind of discouragement around. Feeling like there's even one other person on this planet that values what we're trying to accomplish is enough to turn the corner on discouragement.

If there is someone doing great work, doing something that is amazing, stuff that is admirable or inspiring – tell them. We all need that spark of human connection to help overcome the downward pull of the constant challenge to be amazing, to be way more exciting than yesterday, to do all of that and more – tomorrow. It's a demanding world we live in.

Let's help; let's give each other a push, some support and encouragement to do the work that needs to happen to change our world for the better.

…

Procrastination, discouragement, low self-esteem, personal conflicts. They make it hard to have the openness and transparency that is necessary to fully express inspiration.

Entry-level discouragement begins by making us think we're not worthy to have the time, not competent enough to do good work, or just not "destined" to succeed. All this stuff is illogical and foundationless.

Insidiously stupid.

In the clear light of day it's not hard to see beyond the generic negativity of these claims. But when the emotional climate starts to pull downward, rationality goes with it. We start to believe these suggestions as honest and accurate assessments of ourselves. We fall deeper and deeper into a funk and the reality of clearheaded reason fades.

Every job has its down side, there are always bad days and there are always dirty jobs to do. When I worked at a hardware store, the worst it got was slinging 100-pound bags of concrete off the back of a semi trailer. In the creative world, putting up with this intimidating junk is essentially the same kind of thing:

It's just a bad day. Tomorrow will be better.
…

Static: those places on the radio dial where nothing is happening.

Distractions: completely irrelevant stuff that pulls us away from the core of our vision.

They are all basically just interference, like radio static or noise, that encroaches on the good stuff, makes it hard to see and hear the real music, the brilliant images. It's a fog that lies like a filmy gauze over the lens that turns everything into a fuzzy shadow of aimlessness.

But at a higher elevation, our view, our vision, the saturated colors are always there – the brilliance of lighting, the purity of sounds, the depth of focus hasn't changed.

Apply a filter, a mental algorithm to decode and discard the noise from all the distractions and interference. Plug in and engage an internal noise reduction software – a system that's already built-in to vision – to cut through the clutter – the shrapnel and landmines in the road – and keep focused on the good stuff, focused on moving forward. Use the filter of vision to make all those mental potholes and speed bumps vanish in the peripheral blur of real acceleration.

Personal demons? There are a million or more. They're all just stupid.

The more we accept the uniqueness of our individual identity, the more all this negativity becomes simply irrelevant. Strong identity renders external pressures mute. So don't get pulled down. Don't even go there.

"Shut up 'n play yer guitar."

Baked

Are we there yet? Good question; keep checking.

Deadlines, good. Really?

When there's an actual time frame involved, when there's a hard finish line to make a run for, the work is clear. Get the best work done on time. The main challenge centers on pacing, timing, and making sure all the necessary components are posed to come into place at the right moment. Then hit the GO button. Theoretically, everything works as planned, the pieces come together, people do what they're supposed to – when they're supposed to do it – and stuff gets done. Lots of prep, lots of planning, add in a big chunk of previous experience and expertise, and the stew is going to cook itself. Well, yeah, kinda.

Completion isn't really about the deadline. Completion is about developing finely tuned techniques that can pull everything together at the finish line. And that requires strong interconnected relationships between the participants, precisely skilled people in the right place at the right time, a logical plan based on previous experience and insight, and a willingness of all participants to assume the project's goal as their own.

When the project's vision and objective are clearly stated and shared, the individual commitment of the participants can pull the work together very efficiently.

The success of most of my commercial sessions was a result of this kind of collaboration. The deadlines were tight and cast in stone. Time and money were completely inflexible and everything needed to be accomplished within the allocated parameters.

What made those projects so successful was each individual I worked with was willing to adopt the project's goals and limitations as their own and then do everything they could to contribute to the best completion of the project – within those borders.

Encouraged to contribute beyond the simple lead sheets that I provided, their performances were far better than I could ever have made them if I had resorted to micromanaging the details with obsessively elaborate scores. Each musician gave freely of his or her talent and the results were always amazing.

Deadlines put a nice, easy, external wrapper on the whole endeavor. Time-consuming revisions, rewrites or retakes, and "just one more overdub" can only happen within the confines of the time available. At some point, the deadline arrives and the product ships. And it's done. For better or worse, that's it.

Deadlines exert a compelling influence on self-motivation, too. When time is limited there's an extra level of tension in the room, an extra degree of focus that some people really thrive on. A looming deadline will make me dial in an extra level of intensity as I strive to bring together the often-opposing forces of time and artistic quality.

Deadlines can provoke us to do our best work, the first time. Invariably, absolute deadlines hold a ruler over every aspect of the project, and keep everything in motion towards the release date.

Deadlines. It's a love/hate thing, useful and unavoidable.

Good work is built by inspiration, craft, and skill. It comes together with the cooperation and collaboration of those involved when they are encouraged and feel safe to make those above-and-beyond personal contributions. The practicality and expedience that deadlines demand can help facilitate this kind of collaborative environment.

Deadlines work.

...

But what about stuff that has no deadline?

Open-ended projects are an entirely different creature. Without deadlines, there's flexibility everywhere, as far as the eye can see. But even though it's like a day at the beach, two main things still have to happen: the first is finding the personal motivation to sit down and do the work; the other is knowing when to stop – actually bringing the idea to completion. It should be simple, but it never is.

When there's no deadline, there's no urgency. Without urgency, there's nothing external to generate the energy needed to get started. There's no compelling reason to do anything.

Without deadlines, the inspiration and vision has to come from within the idea itself. Something in the project has to be compelling enough to make getting down to business the most attractive option available. The work needs to be satisfying or rewarding enough to overcome the forces of inertia that mire us in procrastination.

When there is no deadline, there's time – lots and lots of it. There's no pressure, no restrictions, everything's cool.

Well, it's good and bad, actually.

Good, because there's time to explore and experiment, to consider possibilities and alternatives. The results can be entirely new, fresh, and unexpected. The thrill of discovery is inspiring and captivating.

Some stuff just never would have seen the light of day if it had to meet a deadline. The experimentation and discovery that has to take place to find something really new, something as world changing as an electric light or a personal computer just couldn't have happen within the constraints of a commercial system. The work we all do on our startups and our visionary projects needs the flexibility of unlimited time. Research and innovation don't punch a time clock.

Working off the clock is an opportunity to address high levels of detail, to pursue perfection at every stage of the work without constraint. The more intense the work, the more fine the craft, the more details to address.

The opportunity to jump down a rabbit hole without having to be concerned what day or week you'll resurface is enticing indeed. It's pretty interesting down there. "I wonder what this might do?" is not a conventional business model, but it just might lead to something brilliant.

…

And then there's the bad part.

Without a deadline there's time to get into all kinds of trouble. Like blind alleys, U-turns, and unending excursions in directions that are simply irrelevant.

It's mission creep. Without the constraints of time, ideas and concepts just keep flowing. And it can seem exciting to contemplate ever more elaborate permutations on the initial idea. What often happens is that once the project starts to materialize, exciting new possibilities present themselves. The development cycle veers away from actually building the project to trying to determine if this new potential is either the new main road or simply irrelevant, a temporary distraction. With my own work, ideas flow into other related and interconnected ideas. It is often very difficult to see the line between this project and a potential new and different project.

It's hard not to go in many directions all at once.

It seems stupid, but it's an easy trap to get stuck in. Like Alice's adventure, the story just gets stranger and stranger – "curiouser and curiouser" – in increments that are so small and unnoticeable that it all seems very plausible. Until one day a whole lot of time has gone by and the project looks nothing like it was intended. Or, worse, it never got finished because it just faded away.

...

It gets messy, very messy. Once the project starts to materialize, new possibilities present themselves, attractive new possible directions appear. With my own work, ideas flow into other related and interconnected ideas. It is often difficult to know where the line between this project and another potential new and interesting project is drawn.

Why is that so bad? The craft of completion becomes an activity of constantly monitoring direction, of trying to determine if this new potential is the main road to follow or just an interesting detour for another day.

The goal is to take a brilliant idea and realize it into a final form that fulfills its greatness. *And to do it as quickly and as efficiently as possible*. Great work doesn't need to take extraordinary amounts of time. Great work just needs to be exciting and fresh and focused and clear and passionate and tangible.

Laboring over all the critical decisions that constantly need to be made absorbs a lot of time. As a work develops, new potentials, new extensions, and the micro-level details of content all need to be resolved. There are an enormous number of questions to answer, deci-decisions to be made, directions to ponder.

This stuff takes time. And the more intense the work, the more fine the craft, the more time it takes.

A clear sense of the purpose and vision of the work, and an awareness of the voice and context, establishes a guide, a set of criteria, to use to efficiently reduce the time it takes to resolve these kinds of issues. Foundational decisions made at the beginning of the project streamline and align decisions that have to be made throughout the life of the work. Decisions consistently aligned with the initial concept drive the development of the work along a straighter path that results in a final form that is more effectively the outcome of the original intent. And time and resources have not been wasted in the pursuit of directions that are not the primary focus of the project.

Without a deadline, it's hard to move through the development cycle without getting lost or distracted.

Keep focused on the project's initial purpose and vision. And use it as a beacon to guide the project's development.

No deadlines?

Total freedom. And, total responsibility.

Momentum, structure, immediacy, urgency, all have to come from within. And monitoring the relative progression of events needs to remain objective enough that the relativity of time doesn't turn the positive energy of unbridled exploration into an infinite loop of indecisiveness.

...

Deadlines or not, work needs to arrive at the destination dressed up and ready for the party.

It's either a drive-all-night, keep the pedal down, fast lane dash from New York to LA or it's turning off the road into the desert in the dark, without GPS, the cell phone, insurance, or backup. Either way, it's going to be a wild ride – intensely exciting and seriously treacherous.

While it may seem counterintuitive, open-ended time frames are no guarantee that the work will be great. And deadlines alone don't really do it, either.

Great work is the skillful and accurate fulfillment of ideas that are exciting and fresh, focused and clear, and passionate and tangible. Time has a way of eroding the immediacy of those qualities – we just wear down, check out, loose the enthusiasm that sparked the whole thing in the first place. And the energy of the initial inspiration just fades away.

What matters most is stuff needs to get finished. We need to kick this piece out the door so we can get on to the next one.

But the craft of completion isn't something that happens only on the final day. Like every aspect of our craft, it is just one of the ongoing multi-threads of creative work. Monitoring completeness is an ongoing component of the work. At every stage of development and implementation, even before the end is in sight, it's important to know what the project should look like – what it's purpose and function will be – when it has arrived at completion. Consistently monitoring this criterion will help guide the work to an efficient conclusion.

One way I know that a project has jumped off the rails is when the revisions are looking more and more like the original. That's when I know it's assessment time – time to figure out what's wrong and why everything is just moving in circles. Another is when I wake up to the realization that the work is so far removed from the original concept I don't even recognize it. It has become an entirely new thing, and it's time again for a serious personal debriefing.

Getting done has a lot to do with thoroughness and completeness. There's a lot of ways to assess that, but here are a few.

This is how I know when a project is definitely baked:
- Time's up.
- You're honestly satisfied that it is working.
- The mechanics are happy; all the details are right.
- The form is logically realized; the logic is clearly perceptible.
- There is a tangible feeling that it makes sense.
- The materials reflect the purpose.
- The structure reinforces or frames the work's objectives.
- It is a congruent and cohesive statement.
- There is no unintended ambiguity.

- The voice and content are consistent and effective.
- Every possible combination of relationship has been presented.
- All the filler and baloney has been edited away.
- There is nothing more to say.
- Everything that needed to happen, has.

…

At the end of the day, when the project is starting to wrap, how can we tell if it's finished or not? There needs to be some way to know when it's really over. What magic incantation is there for that decision? There has to be something better than just sitting around waiting for the good-bye look.

Back in the day when I recorded in real studios and paid for studio time and session players, going back later to fix things was very expensive. Booking more setup time and bringing in the musicians again was just as expensive as the initial session. Re-dos cost nearly as much as the original session, except they were on my nickel. Fixing things later was a bad, bad, painful thing.

Consequently, whatever was recorded, I pretty much had to live with. And every time I heard the recording, those things that were not quite right or that I wished had been done better, came back and haunted me. They nagged me and made me realize that I needed to find a way to avoid putting myself on the post-production wall of shame.

I learned to take a minute after the last take and ask myself, "Any regrets?" I asked my little inner producer if there was anything I was going to be sorry I hadn't done, anything I was going to wish had been better, anything the client or my own sense of integrity would perceive later as just too lame or stupid. And those things got fixed. Right there. And then it was really done. The project was truly baked.

I could walk away with a feeling that the work was complete and that it expressed a level of quality that was the best of my ability at the moment in time. I could live with that.

After awhile, everyone I worked with on those projects started to do the same thing. Pretty soon we all had the same criteria for calling it a day.

And I still use it, today. It is the ultimate criteria. After all the content is polished shiny bright, the expectations and objectives pushed as far as they can go, and the project is poised on the threshold of a life in the real world, I still ask myself the same thing: any regrets?

And then I let it go.

Keep on keeping on

Real change, creative work, stuff that really matters, isn't easy; but it's worth it.

I have no one to blame.

I went into this expecting a high-maintenance relationship. Complicated and tormented. Unrelenting and demanding. A long slog.

But I figured it would be like any other long-term thing. There would be great days and terrible days, there would be a give and take. But over time there would be a balance; eventually something phenomenal would come along that would make the memory of all those annoying hardships evaporate into thin air.

I expected it to work like this: On one side, the ongoing practice of doing the work, of searching for hard-won solutions, would be pretty much all-consuming. The work would demand brilliance, strength, and an abiding commitment, every day. Day after day.

But there also would be those unbelievably breathtaking moments of renewal, inspiration, excitement, and joy.

And that would be enough. I figured those fantastic sparks of creative energy would be the fuel that would keep the system running for months and even years at a stretch. I expected that the memory of success would outlast – and even overcome – the complications and torture of trying to do creative work in the realm of the real world.

Right?

Well, no. Not really. It didn't work. A buzz only lasts so long.

The work is just too hard and complicated to be powered by something as simple as a few moments of adrenalin rush.

That kind of thing wears out way too fast. And like any drug, the thrill fades with repetition. The search for higher and higher levels of ecstasy leads to places that are devastatingly harmful. We've seen that tragedy happen far too many times.

So don't even go there.

It's just not possible to bridge over the vast frontier of shear hard work with the payoff of a few moments of inspirational bliss.

No, it takes something a lot more powerful than that.

…

Value.

It is the basis upon which we can be unequivocally convinced that the work is worth doing – no matter what comes back in return.

That's the problem with the high-maintenance relationship analogy. The paradigm is all about getting; it's a give and get relationship where the only value is on the receiving side. When I was looking for others to give me the validation I thought I needed to keep working, it was never sufficient – it was never convincing enough to really mean anything over the long haul.

Pursuing an assurance of value from external recognition is opening the entire system to factors that are completely unreliable and without any controllable basis. It's a house of cards, way too fragile and easy to knock down. That kind of belief system is doomed to inadequacy because it's entirely subjective, arbitrary, and inconsistent.

The constant up and down of external forces, with their alternating tendency to either validate or discount the work, became more annoying than the struggle to do the work itself. At that point, paying attention to such reactive responses seemed just stupid and illogical.

Parsing and rationalizing the opinions of others – even friends and loved ones –was always way too emotionally exhausting, anyway. But what really took it down was realizing I was spending more time and effort overcoming the opinions of others than doing the work itself. That was the stupid part.

It was illogical because the stability I was looking for was being based on something completely *unstable* – the opinions of others that are invariably beyond anyone's control. We all know shaping the opinions of others is and forever will be entirely voodoo.

Instead, what's needed is an undeterred conviction that doing the work is important, valuable, and significant – no matter what anyone else ever says or thinks.

An externally biased value system – that was never going to work anyway – needs to be replaced with something unwavering and reliable over the long term. So what is the basis of a conviction that doesn't waver, that doesn't bend in the winds of positive or negative reviews, that doesn't change course every time a new song hits the top of the charts or a new fashion cycle hits the street?

What is the source of a value strong and lasting enough that it can keep the work going for the duration?

Getting there is a 180-degree flip. Rather than looking for validation from others, it's a recognition that validity is inherent in the work and its purpose.

When I realized the only thing that really kept me going was that I could see value in the work myself, on my own terms, I stopped thinking I was in this for the recognition of what other people thought of it. It became clear that the value was embedded in the concept, integral to the idea – the vision, scope, voice, and venue.

The more the validity was expressed by the purpose and implementation of the idea, the less personally responsible I was to convince anyone, including myself, of its value.

The work validates itself.

That's really the only value there ever will be, anyway.

The more I focused on making sure the work was rooted in its purpose, the stronger the work became. The ideas became more intense, more compelling, and the content more precise, more direct, more immediate. The connections were deeper, faster, and more real.

I discovered that the work had a power of its own. It wasn't something I had to make happen. It wasn't subjective anymore.

The value was baked in.

When I started to tap into that power source there was absolutely nothing that could pull my work down. There was nothing more powerful than the strength of the work itself.

We just keep on keeping on,
We just keep on keeping on. – Curtis Mayfield

...
Each idea needs to be expressed and realized. And then pushed out the door and let loose on a world that will discover its value and necessity.

The world is waiting to be convinced and persuaded and shown the real value this idea deserves.

Show them. Even if it's not easy. It's worth it.

The power to do important work, to realize great ideas, and to initiate significant change is the intangible intersection between authenticity, commitment, and respect held in the light of uncompromised value and significance.

Ideas alone are not enough. Ideas must lead. Ideas and creative work propel us all forward into a new day, into new opportunities and new realizations of who we are and what really matters. It's all about the work's ability to improve the experience of real people living real lives.

Change.

Is the world a better place because the work is out there, in the light of day, doing its thing?

Ideas change us. Each one of us.

That really is the only measure.

Epilogue

Flying

It was gravity's fault.

There is no evidence that Leonardo actually got off the ground.

Among the thousands of pages in Leonardo's notebooks are drawings of mechanical wings, and various parts of flying machines. His drawing of the main fuselage with the pedals and pulley system that would move the wings and power the craft appears on the front of page 75 in the set of manuscripts referred to as the *Paris B Codex* (folio 75r). The drawing dates from 1488 or 1489.

He had the vision, the idea, the inspiration – but his creative method wasn't happening. Leonardo's ornithopter didn't fly because his idea never progressed beyond the inspiration stage.

He needed to figure out how to get a heavy wooden and leather airframe powered by a heavy, slow, and proportionally weak human to overcome the pull of gravity. He needed to apply a system, the craft of discovery, development, and implementation to bring his idea to completion.

If he had actually built his ornithopter, he would have realized that it could never fly. He needed to discover that the power-to-weight ratio of a bird far exceeds that of a human. He needed tools like a high-frame-rate video camera to examine just how much energy a bird exerts at the moment it launches into the air. He needed to give up his fascination with bird wings as the source of human flight and focus on how to replicate the extremely fast and strong breast muscles that birds use to launch themselves into the air. He needed to design within the constraints of his available resources – 16th century fabrics and wooden structural members.

And it gets even more complicated than that.

In 1505 on the back cover of *The Codex on the Flight of Birds*, Leonardo wrote, "The great bird will take its first flight from the back of the great [Monte] Ceceri, filling the universe with wonder and all my writings with his fame, and bringing eternal glory to the place where he was born."

Not only does Leonardo want to fly, he wants to be rich and famous, too.

He needed to stay focused on the *purpose* of his initial inspiration and do whatever was necessary to achieve it. If he had been committed to the *craft* of creativity, he would have discovered that the ornithopter – his initial stage of implementation – needed a lot of development work.

He needed to remain open to alternative concepts that achieved the inspiration. And he needed to build it, and *rebuild* it until it worked. He needed to discover the flaws himself, and regroup, draw again, and try again. Over and over.

He needed to search for other means to achieve the fundamental vision of human flight. And in doing so, he also would have accomplished the secondary goal of fame and wealth.

...

Snowbird, designed and built at the University of Toronto, made the first human-powered flight by an ornithopter on August 2, 2010. It maintained altitude and airspeed for 19.3 seconds.

520 years after Leonardo's drawing.

But Snowbird looks nothing like Leonardo's design. It is made of carbon fiber, machined balsa wood, and thin plastic film. And it needs a truck to drag it into the air because it can't take off with human power. That is still just not possible.

Centuries passed before the right mix of tools, knowledge, and materials were available to accomplish Leonardo's vision. But I don't think any of us want to wait around that long for our ideas to see the light of day.

That's why the craft of creativity is so essential. With an understanding that creativity is more than inspiration alone, Leonardo could have discovered the flaws in his idea and found an implementation that could have worked within the context of his time and resources.

He could have built his glider.

And that would have been very cool indeed.

...

Flying.

It requires energy to establish the thrust that actually gets the thing off the ground. It is about making sure the weight of the airframe doesn't absorb all the energy.

It's about applying as much force as possible to the forward motion that actually generates the lift and keeps everything and everyone in the air.

It's knowing when an idea isn't working and the concept needs to go in a completely new direction. Stuff needs to get built and tested and revised and rebuilt and tested again until it actually does what the inspiration intends it to do.

Too often it's easy to think an idea is ready to go right out of the box. It really never is. Inspiration is the beginning. And there's a lot of work and many stages of development and implementation yet to go.

Let's be as enthusiastically inspired as Leonardo but let's also do the work to make stuff happen. Let's fulfill the craft of discovery, development, and implementation and bring the work to completion.

That's the complete span of creativity – an idea made real.

...

The craft of creativity discovers the unknown and transforms it into something real.

Birds soaring upon the wind can inspire us to fly. But it takes more than inspiration to get off the ground.

Our craft reaches out and captures ideas that are entirely new and then molds and shapes them into something tangible, something we all can hold and use. Creativity is a framework, a system that allows us to search and explore without getting lost, to experiment and develop without crashing, and to propel our words and works into the hearts and lives of real people, everywhere.

This is the craft that makes creativity work.

It is this craft of creativity that makes our work happen, minute by minute and year by year. It is micro and macro – the tools and techniques, the structures and relationships that help us put all these strange and wonderful pieces together in a way that has real meaning, purpose, validity, and tangible practical functionality. It is our craft that builds something that actually achieves the vision and potential, that makes the audience laugh, cry, or sing along, that reaches out and inspires, or shows us all the way into a better and fuller life.

If creativity has the power to lift us all higher, it is our craft that activates the idea in a way that generates the motion, that develops the lift that makes the implementation and completion of our vision entirely possible and real.

The work of art is our own individual expression of the craft of creativity. This alone is our guide, the one sure thing amid a life of complete unreason. It is the way we discover how to stand amid the jarring elements of limitation and discouragement and to find a little bit more resolve to keep going. It is the way we find even one more drop of inspiration that will generate that last bit of energy or insight needed to propel an idea fast enough, long enough, to actually lift off the ground.

So take the time, search, experiment, develop, revise, and regroup. Arrive at a system that is built from the ground up upon your own circumstances, your own vision, your own purpose.

Don't stop until it really works.

Such are the arms that hold us and keep us from falling. It is the way our work lifts us all higher.

Creativity, it really is like flying.

Works Cited

"A Study of Da Vinci's Flying Machine" by Qianyu Liu presents a scientific determination on whether human-powered flight would have been possible in this airframe. Accessed August 21, 2013 <http://www.behance.net/gallery/Da-Vincis-Flying-Machine/3875707>.

The Jim Lehrer interview is "A writer for all seasons. Jim Lehrer balances fact with fiction as newsman, novelist, and playwright" by Louise Sweeney, The Christian Science Monitor, August 12, 1987.

Stravinsky's quote is found in Talking Music by William Duckworth, p. 450, published by Da Capo Press, 1999.

An early use of the term parabuilding appeared in "Art/Architecture; A Queens Factory is Born Again, as a Church" by Herbert Muschamp, New York Times, September 5, 1999 accessed January 10, 2014 <http://www.nytimes.com/1999/09/05/arts/art-architecture-a-queens-factory-is-born-again-as-a-church.html?pagewanted=all&src=pm>.

Information on Snowbird, the Human-Powered Ornithopter Project at the University of Toronto accessed November 26, 2013 <http://hpo.ornithopter.net>.

The quote from the inside back cover of Leonardo's The Codex on the Flight of Birds is found in several translations including The Mind of Leonardo da Vinci by Edward McCurdy, p. 279, and accessed November 26, 2013 <http://www.leonardo-to-mars.com/index.php/inside-back-cover.html>. The original Italian is as follows:

"Piglierà il primo volo il grande uccello sopra il dosso del suo grande Cecero, riempiendo l'universo di stupore, riempiendo della sua fama ogni scritto, e gloria eterna al luogo dove nacque.

Keep on Keeping On lyrics by Curtis Mayfield © Copyright Warner/Chappell Music, Inc.

Snowbird photo used by permission.

Other photos courtesy of the author.

From the Author

For as long as I can remember I've been a musician. Rock, jazz, and avant-garde classical. My music compositions have been performed in Europe, Asia, and throughout the US. For nearly as long, I've been a photographer of musicians and the street. My films and writings on creativity and artistic expression are a result of these combined interests. My most recent project was a three-year journey across America to capture the creativity of street musicians in places like New Orleans, San Francisco, and New York.

Throughout the 1980s I was a freelance commercial music producer confronting the intersection between art and commerce at a time when technology was rapidly changing the recording studio landscape.

And for over twenty-five years I was a college professor who taught composition and jazz students how to expand their creativity and discover their personal style. Across all these years, I have served as chair of music, mass communication, and communication departments, and as the division chair of creative arts and communication. Now, I'm Director of Academic Special Programs at a liberal arts college on the bluffs overlooking the Mississippi where I work with faculty to develop multidisciplinary and experiential academic programs.

My other published writings include concert reviews and articles on music technology for magazines and music journals. I am the host of "Creativity Is…" a YouTube series of in-depth interviews of artists and innovators. My wife and I live in a century-old historic home in St. Louis where I use the space to record and produce avant-garde jazz and classical music.

…

Thank you for reading my book. If you enjoyed it, won't you please take a moment to leave me a review at your favorite retailer? And I hope you'll stay in touch. Share your thoughts about creativity and what works for you. I look forward to hearing your ideas!

James Hegarty

www.JimHegarty.com
www.TheCreativeEdgeBooks.com
www.Facebook.com/TheCreativeEdgeBooks
twitter.com/JamesHegarty